The
GREAT
GATSBY

COOKING AND
ENTERTAINING GUIDE

The

GREAT GATSBY

COOKING AND ENTERTAINING GUIDE

Decadent Dishes and Classic Cocktails from the Roaring Twenties

VERONICA HINKE

weldon**owen**

CONTENTS

INTRODUCTION

This collection of historical recipes honors the hundred years since the first copy of *The Great Gatsby* rolled through a printing press. These recipes also celebrate the 1920s, which is the distinct setting of the book. You couldn't buy a drop of liquor, legally, but somehow still the 1920s will forever be known as one of the most jubilant decades in world history. Prohibition didn't seem to deter most. Bathtub gins, backyard stills, downtown and countryside speakeasies, as well as a whole new approach to home entertaining generated celebrations and smiles. Fueled by the prosperity of post-World War I America, the jazz age—as F. Scott Fitzgerald officially dubbed it—was personified as much by the hard-partying pastimes and flowing Champagne as by the glitzy, gold-embossed dishes in which food was often served.

There was much to celebrate. Women had finally received the right to vote. There was greater availability than ever before of fresh fruits and vegetables. There were lifestyle-altering inventions. The expression "the greatest thing since sliced bread" became popular in 1928 when engineer Otto Frederick Rohwedder invented the world's first-ever bread-slicing machine. The decade was marked by significant cultural changes that no one could have ever imagined, with widespread availability of inventions like electricity, the refrigerator, the toaster, the electric knife, and more.

Confidence prevailed. Young people everywhere eagerly demonstrated their endurance in fast-paced roller-skating parties, food-eating contests, kissing marathons, high-energy dances, dance marathons, and more.

The same year that *The Great Gatsby* was published, 1925, the Mayfair Hotel (now the Magnolia Hotel) opened in St. Louis, Missouri. Shortly after, the kitchen staff minted a new sandwich of turkey and ham on toasted white bread. In line with the times, they christened the new menu item the Prosperity Sandwich.

The crisp, clean lines and grand, dramatic designs of the Art Nouveau and Art Deco styles defined the decorative arts of the era. Brightly colored parrots and shimmering iridescent peacocks were frequently depicted in service dishes and home accessories.

In 1929, Leo Reisman and His Orchestra, with vocals by Lou Levin, recorded the song "Happy Days Are Here Again." In 1930, it became the theme song of the movie *Chasing Rainbows* and the anthem of Franklin Delano Roosevelt's presidential campaign.

Happy days were back again, and Americans didn't waste a single second of those

bonus postwar years they'd been granted. In newspapers, etiquette columnists even green-lighted leaving food behind on plates now that wartime rationing was over.

Each of these recipes in this new collection is rooted in the 1920s and honors this very special time capsule in American history. There is an array of fashionable ingredients and menu items, including the very popular alligator pear, which is what avocados were called at the time.

Some recipes, such as Daisy's Lemon Cakes and Julia Arthur Salad, live on because home cooks graciously shared them in their community's daily newspapers. Others are from menus that have been carefully preserved from some of the ritziest hotels in New York City at the time. A few were even temporary home to *The Great Gatsby* author F. Scott Fitzgerald. At the Knickerbocker, he was adored as much for his festive lifestyle as for the $20 bills that he randomly threw to the staff while he partied. At the "Knick," he hunkered down to write his one-act play *Mr. Icky* while he pined for the love of his life, Zelda Sayre. He had met her the year prior, in 1918. After they wed in 1920, they enjoyed parties, special events, and even a few extended stays in luxury hotels the Plaza and the Biltmore.

There are recipes directly from *The Great Gatsby*, including the cold fried chicken that sat in front of Daisy and Tom, with two bottles of ale, but they didn't touch. Other more interpretive recipes, such as Zelda's Applejack Omelet and the fresh tomato sandwiches that she adored, were inspired by what is known of the food preferences and backgrounds of Scott and Zelda.

Recipes are arranged in five sections, including party appetizers (or "glistening hors d'oeuvres" as Fitzgerald describes them); soups, salads, and sides; main courses; desserts; and sips for teetotalers as well as for tipplers. The recipes are arranged into five examples of menus for parties and special meals, and they can be rearranged to create even more menus for any occasion. Throughout, there are historical references to the narrative of the book as well as what is known of Scott and Zelda and their drinking and dining preferences.

Plan a movie night or host a book club gathering with this assortment as a guide for what to serve. Whether with a romantic picnic for two or a large summer party, acknowledge and celebrate a hundred years of one of the greatest American novels.

PROHIBITION

How One Law Created a Time Capsule in Drinking and Dining History

Prohibition was an unprecedented time in the history of the United States. From 1920 to 1933, U.S. law prohibited the manufacture, sale, or transport of liquor of any kind. It was harder than ever to make boeuf bourguignon or coq au vin in your own kitchen. Societal norms were broken and challenged irrevocably by the new legislation.

The law did not stop home cooks and party hosts. In fact, it encouraged home entertaining, which inspired whole new styles, innovations, and designs of serving dishes (see Dining and Entertaining, page 11). For example, the new concepts of shrimp cocktail and fruit cocktail emerged as a way of repurposing cocktail glasses for serving food instead of mixed drinks.

Just as pre-Prohibition is a distinct time capsule in drinking and dining history, Prohibition is a time period that is marked by its own trends. Pre-Prohibition drinks like the Clover Club, the Robert Burns, the Rob Roy, and the Bronx were lost, at least for many years, at the start of Prohibition. In recent years, the painstaking research of mixologists and cocktail historians has helped put these cocktails back on menus. The cocktails they gave way to, those that emerged during Prohibition, just as distinctly define an era. The Gin Rickey (see the recipe with a modern twist of fresh lavender on page 105), the French 75, and more cocktails became some of the most popular drinks of the 1920s. Many of the new drinks, which were mostly gin-based because it was easiest to make gin in home distilleries ("bathtub gin"), had names that reflected the carefree whimsy of the time. The Bee's Knees, which is made with a touch of honey (page 106), is one of the best examples.

LITERARY SIGNIFICANCE

The Great Gatsby: *A Beacon of Hope*

Four days before Christmas in 1940, F. Scott Fitzgerald for the last time closed his eyes on the world over which they had oversight like the watchful eyes of his billboard character, Doctor Eckleburg. He was forty-four. He was never able to enjoy the sensation that his book stirred: In the fifteen years prior to his passing, reception of *The Great Gatsby* was dismal and sales were scant after it was published.

However, since its first publication a hundred years ago, in 1925, more than 30 million copies of this classic American novel have been sold. The book has inspired four blockbuster movies. Each year still, some 500,000 copies are purchased. Why does *The Great Gatsby* continue to grip the hearts of people everywhere?

Just shortly after Fitzgerald passed away, another world war began to shroud the globe in a fresh blanket of uncertainty and fear. A kind of anxiety was produced that sent people seeking relief and, in pre-television, pre-internet America, for most people that came in the form of literature. Set in the carefree days of the jubilant post-WWI New York City area, *The Great Gatsby* was a perfect read. Suddenly, people everywhere heartily embraced the little 200-page book that was Fitzgerald's posthumous gift of hope. His message: Happy days will be here again. Almost like nonfiction, Fitzgerald documented and connected people with the high-spirited, celebratory lifestyle that was prevalent in the 1920s in a way that no other book had and may not ever again.

But there were more reasons the book became an American treasure. Like his 1922 short story "The Curious Case of Benjamin Button," which is another exceptional account of fiction that also later inspired an Oscar-winning movie adaptation, *The Great Gatsby* is a prolific narrative told in impressive conciseness while still managing to deftly touch on multiple complicated aspects of human nature.

The Great Gatsby was the first piece of literature to so successfully cross social boundaries, connecting us and allowing us to share in the lives of the haves as much as the have-nots, the richest and the poorest. Fitzgerald provides unparalleled access into each character's innermost thoughts and feelings. We have a seat at the table of individuals and families of all walks of life in the 1920s.

At the same time, Fitzgerald illuminates the American dream, questioning and

continued on page 10

continued from page 9

weighing out whether it applies fairly to everyone. Gatsby dreams of attaining social acceptance from the old wealth of New York, making the point that even the richest of the rich can fall short of their ambitions. More than anything else, though, he dreams of winning the heart of the love of his life, Daisy Buchanan.

Because Daisy is a long-lost love, the story also addresses the ever-important lesson to leave the past behind and move on to the future. Gatsby struggles to move forward with his life without Daisy, which ends up ultimately claiming his life.

Fitzgerald also explores feminism, dropping clues about the role of jazz-era women in the way they dressed, worked, and socialized and how they were limited in social and family structures. Daisy confides that she hopes her daughter will become a "fool" so that she will be prone to fit in with societal norms. What she confesses might not be as freely stated by other women at the time, but the sentiment was likely shared.

The secret of why *The Great Gatsby* remains a cherished piece of American literature lies in so many aspects, but perhaps the strongest element is in the theme of hope that is represented. We have a front-row seat to the hopes of each character, which allows us to connect with them organically and easily. Throughout his story, Fitzgerald acknowledges this by referencing the constant ball of green light (see recipe on page 120) that glows from a dock in the peaceful waters of the Long Island Sound. He wrote: "Gatsby believed in the green light, the orgiastic future that year-by-year recedes before us. It eluded us then, but that's no matter—tomorrow we will run faster, stretch out our arms farther."

We will try again tomorrow. We will try again the next day and on into the future, hoping that Fitzgerald might somehow realize how his valued masterpiece continues to inspire hope for so many.

DINING AND ENTERTAINING

Prohibition ushered in a whole new brand of style and new approaches to entertaining, which was opulent and dazzling.

Much of the new style was evident in the distinct approach to floral arrangements, which were everywhere. Gold and black luster-covered vases overflowed with ostrich feathers, and iridescent peacock feathers of blue, green, and lavender mixed with Asiatic lilies, phalaenopsis orchids, lavender, and wisteria. In some arrangements, fruits were intermixed with foliage in black, chrome, and silver vases. In handheld bouquets, tendrils and ribbons hung from both ends in a distinct style.

As home entertaining increased, so did new designs in serving dishes and utensils. Many were gold-embossed to reflect the excessive lifestyle of the times. There were new trays and carts for serving cocktails and food. Decorative tea and coffee sets included a coffee urn or a teapot with a cream and sugar set plus a tray for presenting refreshments to multiple guests at once.

For parties there were new designs in cheese-and-cracker and condiment serving sets. Three-piece serving sets for mayonnaise and other condiments included a small pedestal bowl, a ladle, and a plate for the bowl. Hotakold jugs were new thermal serving inventions that kept hot liquids hot and cold liquids cold.

As availability of electricity increased, so did electrical appliances like electric coffee percolators, which were kept plugged in throughout a party to keep the coffee hot. On buffets and consoles, hostesses displayed candelabras and console sets, which included serving bowls and matching candlesticks.

Sets of up to seventy-five elaborate pieces of silverware were kept in handsome rectangular wooden chests about the size of a briefcase. The silver required hours and hours of polishing between each use. Some chests came with a tomato server, berry spoon, special meat forks, and more. There were special dishes for serving lemon wedges, almonds, and eggs.

Smoking stands with multiple receptacles for ashes and indentations where cigarettes could be set to rest accommodated small groups at parties. It was not uncommon to see smoking stands permanently set in living rooms and dens.

GLISTENING HORS D'OEUVRES

"On buffet tables, garnished with glistening hors-d'oeuvres..." —CHAPTER 3

GATSBY'S PASTRY PIGS WITH GRAPE JELLY AND MINT

"There was music from my neighbor's house through the summer nights. On buffet tables…pastry pigs and turkeys bewitched to a dark gold." —CHAPTER 3

These pastry pigs—or "pigs in blankets" as they are also called—are cocktail sausages baked in pastry dough with cream cheese mixed with grape jelly. They are satisfying and delicious bites that are fun to eat. While they are a traditional English holiday party food, they are enjoyed just as much at a moonlit summer pool party. Arrange these on a serving platter with chopped garden mint sprinkled on top for an extra layer of fresh flavor.

YIELD: 32 pastry pigs

1 cup cream cheese, softened

1¼ cups chopped fresh mint, divided

1 teaspoon fresh lemon juice

¼ teaspoon salt

¼ teaspoon sugar

One 1-pound package frozen pastry dough

1 cup Concord grape jelly

One 14-ounce container miniature smoky sausages

1 egg white

Preheat the oven to 350°F. Line a 9-by-12-inch baking sheet with parchment paper.

In a small bowl using a handheld mixer or in a stand mixer, mix the cream cheese, 1 cup of the mint, lemon juice, salt, and sugar until well combined, 1 to 2 minutes. Set aside.

Using a knife, cut the pastry sheets into 2-by-2-inch squares. The pastry is easier to cut while it is frozen.

Spread 1 teaspoon of the cream cheese mixture across each pastry square. Spread 1 teaspoon of the grape jelly across the cream cheese.

Place a sausage diagonally across each of the pastry squares. Use your fingertips to pinch together the upper left corner and the lower right corner of each of the pastry squares. Place the pastries on the prepared baking sheet.

Using a fork, beat the egg white in a small bowl for about 30 seconds. Use a pastry brush to lightly brush the egg white on top of the pastries.

Bake until pastries are golden brown all around, 35 to 40 minutes. Remove from the oven.

When the pastries are cool enough to touch, arrange them on a serving platter, and scatter the remaining ¼ cup chopped mint on top for garnish. Serve immediately.

Store in an airtight container in the refrigerator for 3 to 4 days.

BAKED WEST EGG OYSTERS ROCKEFELLER

"We backed up to a gray old man who bore an absurd resemblance to John D. Rockefeller. In a basket swung from his neck cowered a dozen very recent puppies of an indeterminate breed." —CHAPTER 2

John D. Rockefeller was one of the richest men in the world in 1889 when Jules Alciatore named his new recipe for rich oysters—smothered in bread crumbs, spinach, and butter—after him. Jules was the son of Antoine Alciatore, owner of Antoine's in New Orleans.

Jay Gatsby's estate was in a fictional town called West Egg. The town was based on Great Neck, New York, which is located on Long Island, where today there are more than a dozen oyster farms. Blue Point oysters have been harvested since the early 1800s in Great South Bay, 50 miles southeast of Great Neck.

These oysters can be baked, broiled, or grilled. When serving them, steady the oyster shells by nestling them in coarse sea salt. Safe handling of oysters is very important.

YIELD: 10 servings

1¾ pounds coarse sea salt

1 tablespoon butter

1 large shallot, diced

1 clove garlic, minced

1 large red pepper, cored and diced

3 cups chopped fresh spinach

¼ cup cognac

¼ teaspoon pink Himalayan sea salt

¼ teaspoon freshly ground multicolor peppercorns

10 fresh oysters in the shell

1 large lemon, cut into quarters

2 tablespoons plain bread crumbs

½ cup chopped fresh parsley

Safe handling of oysters is very important. See "Handling Oysters" (page 18).

Preheat the oven to 400°F. Line a 9-by-12-inch shallow baking sheet with parchment paper and spread the coarse salt on top.

In a large frying pan over medium heat, melt the butter. Add the shallot and garlic and stir with a spatula. When the shallot becomes translucent, add the red pepper and spinach and stir to combine. Add the cognac, sea salt, and ground pepper. Continue to cook until the spinach is wilted, 3 to 5 minutes. Set aside.

Wearing thick gloves, shuck the oysters. Separate the top and bottom shells by inserting a sharp knife in the hinge of the oyster. Pry the knife all around the seam, wiggling it to separate the top and bottom halves. Run a knife under the oyster to cut the cord that attaches the meat to the shell. Arrange the oysters on the prepared baking sheet, nestling them into the coarse salt.

Squeeze the fresh lemon juice of one lemon quarter over the oysters. Place 1 tablespoon of the spinach mixture on top of each oyster, then sprinkle with the bread crumbs. Bake until the bread crumbs start to brown, 15 to 20 minutes. Remove from the oven.

Use a large spoon to transfer the salt from the baking sheet to a serving platter. Arrange the oysters in the salt.

Arrange the remaining lemon quarters around the oysters on the platter. Sprinkle with the fresh parsley.

HANDLING OYSTERS

- Place a thick glove or cloth over the hand that is holding the oyster as it is shucked.

- Locate the hinge of the oyster using the tip of the oyster knife. Insert the knife in it, and slide the knife back and forth slightly. Pry the shell open by pushing the knife downward.

- When the oyster is open, disconnect the meat from the shell by sliding the knife between the meat and the shell.

- Allow plenty of time to avoid injury due to rushing. Oysters can be shucked about one hour before guests arrive.

- Arrange them in a serving dish filled with ice, and cover them until time to serve. Keep oysters on ice at all times.

- The National Institute of Food and Agriculture provides this safety fact sheet online: https://www.nifa.usda.gov/sites/default/files/resource/MolluscanShellfishSafetyAndQuality.pdf

SWEDISH MEATBALLS WITH LINGONBERRY SAUCE

YIELD: About 50 meatballs, depending on size

MEATBALLS

8 ounces ground pork

8 ounces ground beef

3 tablespoons whole milk

1 egg

½ cup crushed rich butter crackers

½ cup diced red bell pepper

¼ cup chopped celery

1 tablespoon chopped fresh parsley, plus more for garnish

½ teaspoon minced garlic

1 teaspoon minced shallot

¼ teaspoon allspice

¼ teaspoon nutmeg

¼ teaspoon mustard powder

¼ teaspoon black pepper

¼ teaspoon salt

SWEDISH MEATBALL SAUCE

1 tablespoon butter

1 tablespoon all-purpose flour

2 cups heavy cream

2 cups chicken broth

¼ teaspoon nutmeg

¼ teaspoon allspice

¼ teaspoon salt

¼ teaspoon freshly ground multicolor peppercorns

LINGONBERRY-MINT DIPPING SAUCE

2 cups lingonberry jam

½ cup chopped fresh mint

¼ teaspoon salt

The Great Gatsby author F. Scott Fitzgerald was born in St. Paul, Minnesota, in 1896. At the time, his family lived on the second floor of an apartment building at 481 Laurel Avenue. Two years later, his family moved to Buffalo, New York. The Fitzgeralds returned to St. Paul in 1908, and they lived for two years in a rowhouse at 286-294 Laurel Avenue. In summer 1919, Fitzgerald finished his novel, This Side of Paradise, *while staying with his parents at 599 Summit Avenue in St. Paul.*

These meatballs reflect Minnesota's distinct Swedish heritage. Freshly grated nutmeg and allspice add warm notes to a thick, creamy white sauce. A touch of mustard powder brightens the flavor. A sauce made of jam packed with delicate, pretty red lingonberries provides a sweet and tart topping for each bite.

Serve these on a platter, as a passed appetizer, or on a buffet, or over fluffy mashed potatoes for a meal. Hearty bites like these were simmering on stove tops all around as Fitzgerald was growing up.

Preheat the oven to 350°F. Line a 9-by-12-inch baking sheet with parchment paper.

To make the meatballs: Place all of the ingredients in a large mixing bowl. Use one hand to mix the ingredients together until they are just combined.

Use a small melon baller or a small ice cream scoop to make 1-inch balls with the meat mixture. Roll each piece in your hands to make a smooth, round ball. Place the balls 2 inches apart on the prepared baking sheet. Bake until golden brown and the meat reaches 160°F in the center, 45 to 50 minutes. Remove the meatballs from the oven.

To make the Swedish meatball sauce: In a large frying pan over medium-high heat, melt the butter. Use a large spoon to stir in the flour until it becomes slightly nutty smelling and is blended in thoroughly with the butter. Add the cream, broth, nutmeg, allspice, salt, and pepper; stir to combine. Let the sauce simmer until thickened, about 30 minutes. Stir occasionally. Add the meatballs, and let the meatballs simmer in the sauce for 10 minutes.

To make the dipping sauce: In a large mixing bowl, combine the lingonberry jam, mint, and salt. Use a spoon to mix the ingredients together well. Place the sauce in a serving bowl and set it alongside the meatballs on a plate or platter. Garnish with parsley.

WALDORF SALAD BITES

By the time F. Scott Fitzgerald began frequenting some of the most flamboyant New York City hotels like the Waldorf-Astoria in early 1920s, the Waldorf salad was already a favorite of the well-heeled Manhattan crowd. The salad was created at the Waldorf-Astoria by Executive Chef Edouard Beauchamp and Mâitre d'Hôtel Oscar Tschirky in 1893. With its fresh apples and grapes, tangy dressing, and pops of lightly toasted walnuts, the salad quickly took hold as a restaurant trend.

A bit of fresh tarragon sprinkled on top gives this Waldorf salad a modern flavor twist. While Waldorf salad is usually served on a salad plate, for a pretty passed appetizer, chop the apples and grapes extra-fine and fill large leaves of Belgian endive. Balance the endive leaves on a platter by first arranging variegated radicchio leaves. Wait to add the walnuts until just before serving to ensure they remain crisp.

YIELD: 12 servings

DRESSING

1 cup mayonnaise

1 teaspoon lemon juice

¼ teaspoon paprika

¼ teaspoon salt

¼ teaspoon pepper

¼ teaspoon sugar

SALAD

2 large Honeycrisp apples, skins on, cored and chopped

2 cups green grapes, sliced in half

1 cup diced celery

1 cup toasted walnuts, roughly chopped

1 small head radicchio

5 small heads Belgian endive

1 tablespoon chopped fresh tarragon

To make the dressing: In a large mixing bowl, use a whisk to combine the mayonnaise, lemon juice, paprika, salt, pepper, and sugar.

To make the salad: Add the apples, grapes, celery, and walnuts to the dressing in the bowl and mix gently. Separate the radicchio leaves and arrange them on a serving platter. Tear leaves as needed. Separate the largest, hardiest leaves from the endive heads. Fill each leaf with 2 tablespoons of the salad. Arrange the endive leaves on the bed of radicchio. Sprinkle the tarragon on top.

COLD CRAB DIP

▽

Peter Cooper obtained the first U.S. patent for a gelatin cooking powder in 1845, but it wasn't until the 1920s that the powder caught on as a national culinary craze. Gelatin powder was in almost every American kitchen in a rainbow of colored and fruit-flavored varieties.

This cold crab dip is made with plain gelatin that holds all of the ingredients together. It is similar to the delights that would have been served at 1920s cocktail parties. It has a seafood flavor with a little bit of punch from a few drops of Worcestershire sauce and a heavy sprinkle of hot Hungarian paprika. Finely chopped celery and leaves, chives, and thyme introduce modern flavors in this variation of the classic recipe. Sprinkle some finely chopped celery leaves, diced red bell pepper, and chives on top for color. Fresh lemon juice makes it fresh and bright.

YIELD: 20 servings

Three 10.5-ounce cans cream of mushroom soup

One 8-ounce package cream cheese, softened

1 cup mayonnaise

2½ teaspoons plain gelatin

¼ cup hot water

1 teaspoon Worcestershire sauce

2 tablespoons chopped celery, including some leaves, plus more leaves for garnish

Three 6-ounce cans white crabmeat, drained and rinsed

1 large red bell pepper, cored and minced

1 large shallot, minced

1 clove garlic, minced

1 tablespoon hot Hungarian paprika, plus more for garnish

¼ teaspoon pink Himalayan sea salt

¼ teaspoon freshly ground pepper

1 large lemon, cut into quarters, for garnish

1 teaspoon fresh chopped chives, for garnish

Rich butter crackers, for serving

SPECIALTY TOOLS

Copper gelatin mold or a parchment paper-lined 9-by-4-inch bread loaf pan

Butter a copper gelatin mold and set aside.

In a medium saucepan over medium heat, combine the cream of mushroom soup, cream cheese, and Worcestershire sauce. Stir occasionally until blended and smooth. Remove from the heat and stir in the mayonnaise.

In a medium bowl, combine the gelatin powder and hot water. Let this sit until the gelatin dissolves, 4 to 6 minutes.

Add the gelatin to the soup mixture. Mix in the celery, crab, bell pepper, shallot, garlic, paprika, salt, and pepper. Squeeze one lemon quarter into the mixture, and stir until combined.

Pour the mixture into the prepared mold. Place in the refrigerator to set for at least 4 hours, best if overnight.

When ready to serve, place a serving platter on top of the copper mold and invert the mold onto the platter. If the crab dip does not release from the copper mold, place hot water in a container that is larger than the copper mold. Hold the mold in the hot water for 30 to 40 seconds.

Arrange the remaining lemon quarters around the crab dip. Garnish with chives and additional celery leaves and paprika. Serve with rich butter crackers.

CREAMY PESTO-STUFFED CELERY

Celery was served in a special "celery dish" on every fashionable Victorian and Edwardian table. In the 1920s, the trend of serving celery sticks stuffed with creamy cheeses, peanut butter, and other spreadable treats caught on like the Lindy Hop.

Chop the pretty, delicate celery leaves finely and sprinkle on top to add contrasting color, texture, and flavor. Try serving celery sticks stuffed with two or three different fillings. This recipe features a more modern ingredient, basil, which tastes like a summer garden on the Long Island Sound.

These celery bites are a cinch to make and add pops of color to a buffet table or serving tray loaded with party appetizers. Cut into 2-inch pieces, they can easily be eaten in two or three bites.

YIELD: 24 servings

8 stalks celery

2 cups cream cheese, softened

1 cup pesto

1 teaspoon fresh lemon juice

¼ teaspoon pink Himalayan sea salt

¼ teaspoon freshly ground multicolor peppercorns

⅛ teaspoon sugar

5 or 6 celery hearts and leaves (the innermost celery sticks), chopped, for garnish

¼ cup diced red bell pepper

Clean and trim the celery stalks and cut each into three pieces.

In a bowl using a handheld mixer or in a stand mixer, mix the cream cheese, pesto, lemon juice, salt, ground pepper, and sugar until well combined. Using a knife, spread the mixture into each of the pieces of celery. Arrange the celery sticks on a serving platter.

Scatter the chopped celery hearts and leaves across the celery sticks, and sprinkle the red bell pepper on top for garnish.

DEVILED FOODS

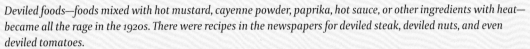

Deviled foods—foods mixed with hot mustard, cayenne powder, paprika, hot sauce, or other ingredients with heat—became all the rage in the 1920s. There were recipes in the newspapers for deviled steak, deviled nuts, and even deviled tomatoes.

Some of the most popular deviled party foods were deviled lobster, deviled ham, and deviled eggs. To celebrate these foods that are still favorites today, arrange an assortment of them on a serving tray to pass at a party. Fill tiny leaves of Belgian endive with a tablespoon of deviled lobster. Roll deviled ham into bite-size balls and set each ball on a thin slice of cucumber. Fill hard-boiled egg whites with creamy deviled egg yolk mixture. Place deviled olives throughout the tray. Sprinkle just a touch of very finely diced hot peppers or hot paprika on top of the deviled foods. These can also be served in a bowl as a spread for toast points or crackers.

DEVILED LOBSTER BITES

YIELD: 20 servings

1 pound lobster meat

1 cup mayonnaise

½ teaspoon paprika, plus more for garnish

1 tablespoon fresh lemon juice

¼ teaspoon sea salt

¼ teaspoon freshly ground black pepper

1 English cucumber

10 fresh chives, cut into 1-inch pieces

In a large mixing bowl, combine the lobster, mayonnaise, paprika, lemon juice, salt, and pepper. Using your hands, mix until all of the ingredients are well combined.

Slice the cucumber into ½-inch-thick slices. Place 1 tablespoon of the lobster on top of each cucumber slice. Arrange on a serving platter and garnish with a sprinkle of paprika and the chives.

Opposite page, top to bottom:
Deviled Ham Balls, recipe page 28
Deviled Eggs, recipe page 28
Deviled Lobster Bites, recipe this page
Deviled Olives, recipe page 29

DEVILED HAM BALLS

YIELD: 20 servings

1 pound ground ham

1 cup mayonnaise

½ cup hot spicy mustard

½ teaspoon paprika, plus more for garnish

¼ teaspoon sea salt

¼ teaspoon freshly ground black pepper

1 English cucumber

¼ cup chopped fresh parsley

In a large mixing bowl, combine the ham, mayonnaise, mustard, paprika, salt, and pepper. Using your hands, mix until all of the ingredients are well combined. Roll the mixture into 1-inch balls.

Slice the cucumber into ½-inch-thick slices. Set a ham ball on top of each cucumber slice.

Arrange on a serving platter and garnish with a sprinkle of paprika and the fresh parsley.

DEVILED EGGS

YIELD: 24 servings

24 large eggs

2 cups mayonnaise

½ cup Dijon mustard

½ teaspoon hot sauce

1 teaspoon paprika, plus more for sprinkling

¼ teaspoon sea salt

½ teaspoon freshly ground multicolor peppercorns

1 head oakleaf lettuce, leaves separated

¼ cup chopped fresh parsley

Place the eggs in a large heavy saucepan over high heat, add water to cover by 1 to 2 inches, and bring to a boil. Reduce heat to medium and boil until eggs are solid, about 8 to 10 minutes. Remove from the heat, cover, and let stand for 15 minutes. Transfer the eggs to a bowl of ice water and let stand for 15 minutes to stop the cooking. Peel the eggs. Halve each egg lengthwise. Remove the yolk from each egg, being careful not to break the whites, placing the yolks in a large bowl. Set the whites aside.

Using a fork, mash the yolks. Add the mayonnaise, mustard, hot sauce, paprika, salt, and pepper and mix until thoroughly combined. Transfer the egg yolk filling to a pastry bag fitted with a large round tip. Alternatively, you can use a large plastic storage bag with ½ inch of a bottom corner cut off. Roll the sides of the bag down so that you can fill it at the open end. Fill the bag with the mixture, roll the sides back up, and press the mixture into the open corner.

Line a large platter with the lettuce leaves. Arrange the egg whites around the platter on top of the lettuce leaves. Pipe the filling into the wells of the egg whites. Garnish with a sprinkle of paprika and the fresh parsley.

DEVILED OLIVES

▽

YIELD: 20 servings

One 8.5-ounce container large pimento-stuffed olives, drained

1½ tablespoons extra-virgin olive oil

1 tablespoon dried red pepper flakes

1 clove garlic, roughly chopped

In a medium mixing bowl, combine the olives, olive oil, red pepper flakes, and garlic. Cover the mixture and place in the refrigerator for 4 to 5 days. Stir the olives every day. Transfer to a serving bowl and let come to room temperature before serving.

QUICK PICKLED CARROTS

▽

Pickling was a popular culinary technique in the 1920s. Carrots, green beans, cucumbers, beets, and more—even watermelon rind—could be stored for months on pantry shelves in canning jars after being "pickled." These items are wonderful for munching on at parties and can be a cocktail garnish.

There are three types of pickling: salt-brine pickling, vinegar-brine soak and rinse pickling, and quick pickling. Quick pickling is an option for putting together last-minute party bites that add a variety of flavors and textures. There is nothing like the pop of a freshly pickled vegetable. Wash and cut a favorite vegetable, and then place the pieces in a dish and cover them with vinegar and spices. Set the dish in the refrigerator until the vegetables soften but still have a bit of crunch, about 3 to 4 hours for best results. One hour is enough time to pickle if necessary.

YIELD: 12 servings

16 large carrots, trimmed and peeled

1 cup water

1 cup white wine vinegar

1 cup sugar

6 juniper berries

2 bay leaves

1 tablespoon pickling spice

¼ teaspoon sea salt

¼ teaspoon freshly ground black pepper

Using a knife, julienne the carrots by cutting them into 3-inch-long sticks.

In a medium bowl, combine the water, vinegar, sugar, juniper berries, bay leaves, pickling spice, salt, and pepper. Add the carrots and make sure the liquid covers them. Cover the bowl and place in the refrigerator for at least 3 to 4 hours or overnight.

SHRIMP COCKTAIL

Icy shrimp served with a cold tomato sauce—a "cocktail sauce" or "seafood sauce"—is called a shrimp cocktail. Cocktail sauces became popular in the late 1800s. Most varieties were ketchup or tomato sauce mixed with mayonnaise or a little horseradish and some fresh lemon juice. By 1920, recipes for homemade cocktail sauces began appearing in newspapers.

Serve two or three shrimp for each guest in a pretty martini glass lined with a little piece of iceberg lettuce. Place a few small pieces of fresh lemon and sprinkle bits of fresh bright green parsley across the top. For those who like a spicier bite, flake some horseradish on top of the cocktail sauce.

Pass shrimp cocktails on a tray or set them out on a table mixed with other party appetizers.

**YIELD: 8 servings
(3 shrimp per serving)**

2 pounds (24 pieces)
frozen jumbo shrimp

4 cups ketchup

½ cup coarse-cut horseradish,
plus more for garnish

2 tablespoons
Worcestershire sauce

1 tablespoon hot sauce

2 lemons, 1 juiced, the
other cut into wedges

8 small iceberg or butter lettuce
leaves, for lining glasses

½ cup chopped fresh parsley

Freshly ground multicolor
peppercorns

Transfer the shrimp from the freezer to the refrigerator for 3 hours to thaw. Rinse the shrimp under cold water while peeling and pulling off the tails.

In a medium mixing bowl, mix together the ketchup, horseradish, Worcestershire sauce, hot sauce, and lemon juice until well combined.

Place a lettuce leaf in each of the glasses. Fill each glass three-fourths full of the cocktail sauce and arrange three shrimp around the rim of each glass, with their tail end hanging over the side. Garnish with a lemon wedge and a sprinkle of fresh parsley. Top each shrimp cocktail with a dab of horseradish and a sprinkle of freshly ground black pepper.

BACON AND HORSERADISH CHEESEBALL

A cheeseball would have been a centerpiece at practically any cocktail party in the 1920s. The fun of making this is in rolling the ball of softened cheese in tasty bits of chopped bacon, nuts, fresh herbs, or spices.

Select soft cheeses from F. Scott Fitzgerald's home state of Minnesota, where some of the best cheeses in the world are made. Try combining a few varieties of contrasting colors of cheeses, such as mixing soft Cheddar with blue cheese or white cream cheese. Do the same with the outer ingredients that make the coating around the cheeseball.

Cheeseballs can be made a few days before a party if they are kept in the refrigerator. They can even taste better after a day or two. They can also be kept in the freezer for a few months, which is nice for holiday parties.

YIELD: 20 servings

One 8-ounce block sharp Cheddar cheese, grated

Two 8-ounce packages cream cheese, softened

One 12-ounce package bacon, prepared according to instructions on the package and chopped

2 teaspoons Worcestershire sauce

1 teaspoon mustard powder

½ cup coarse-cut horseradish

1 clove garlic, minced

¼ teaspoon sea salt

¼ teaspoon freshly ground multicolor peppercorns

1 cup walnuts

In a large mixing bowl, combine the Cheddar cheese, cream cheese, half of the bacon, the Worcestershire sauce, mustard powder, horseradish, garlic, salt, and pepper. Using your hands, mix until all of the ingredients are well combined. Roll the mixture into a ball.

Using a large knife or a nut chopper, chop the walnuts. Spread the walnuts and remaining bacon evenly on the countertop. Roll the cheeseball all around in the nuts and bacon mixture so that the ball is evenly covered.

Cover the cheeseball with plastic wrap. Store in the refrigerator for 5 to 7 days. Store in the freezer for 2 to 3 months.

SMOKED WHITEFISH DIP

"She was appalled by West Egg, this unprecedented 'place' that Broadway had begotten upon a Long Island fishing village—appalled by its raw vigor that chafed under the old euphemisms and by the too obtrusive fate that herded its inhabitants along a short-cut from nothing to nothing. She saw something awful in the very simplicity she failed to understand." —CHAPTER 6

This recipe for this dip brings the flavor of Jay Gatsby's West Egg and celebrates the legacy of the storied fishing village. Form the dip into a large ball, and serve it surrounded by bread and crackers on a tray or smeared on individual bite-size pieces of bread or crackers. Buy smoked fish from the fish shop or try smoking it in a smoker at home.

YIELD: 20 servings

The meat from one 3-pound smoked whitefish

1½ cups mayonnaise

2 teaspoons Worcestershire sauce

1 teaspoon paprika

¼ teaspoon freshly ground multicolor peppercorns

2 lemons, 1 juiced, the other cut into wedges

½ cup chopped fresh dill

Remove the meat from the bones of the whitefish, and place it in a medium mixing bowl. Using a fork, flake the fish meat.

In a bowl using a handheld mixer or in a stand mixer, add the fish, mayonnaise, Worcestershire sauce, paprika, pepper, and lemon juice and mix until well combined. Place in a serving bowl and place the bowl on a platter with crackers, baguette slices, or toast points. Garnish with the lemon wedges and fresh dill.

SOUPS, SALADS, AND SIDES

42ND STREET CELLAR "SUCCULENT" HASH

"A succulent hash arrived, and Mr. Wolfsheim, forgetting the more sentimental atmosphere of the old Metropole, began to eat with ferocious delicacy. His eyes, meanwhile, roved very slowly all around the room—he completed the arc by turning to inspect the people directly behind. I think that, except for my presence, he would have taken one short glance beneath our own table." —CHAPTER 4

This potato dish is as satisfying as the hash that Mr. Wolfsheim eagerly devoured for lunch at "a well-fanned Forty-second Street cellar." In the Roaring Twenties, one of the most popular side dishes was potatoes au gratin. Use a mandoline slicer to slice the potatoes paper-thin, which is the secret to the best potatoes au gratin.

A generous sprinkle of hot Hungarian paprika helps create a lightly crispy coating on top of these potatoes. Underneath the browned topping is a rich, creamy filling.

YIELD: 8 to 10 servings

3 tablespoons salted butter

3 tablespoons all-purpose flour

2 cups heavy cream

1 teaspoon sea salt

¼ teaspoon freshly ground black pepper

1 teaspoon chopped fresh lemon thyme, divided

1 cup grated Cheddar cheese

5 large potatoes, unpeeled, finely sliced using a mandoline

1 large red onion, diced

1 large red bell pepper, diced

1 large green bell pepper, diced

1 tablespoon hot Hungarian paprika

Preheat the oven to 375°F. Butter a 9-by-12-inch baking dish.

In a large saucepan over medium-low heat, melt the butter. Add the flour and cook, stirring, for 2 to 3 minutes. Add the cream, salt, ground pepper, and half of the lemon thyme. Bring to a boil, and then decrease to a simmer. Cook, stirring, until combined and smooth.

Remove the saucepan from the stove top and add the cheese, stirring until it is melted. Add in the potatoes, onion, and bell peppers and stir well to combine. Pour the mixture into the prepared baking dish. Sprinkle the paprika and remaining lemon thyme on top.

Cover with foil and bake until the potatoes are tender, about 45 minutes. Remove from the oven and let cool slightly. Use a large serving spoon to serve. Place a fresh sprig of lemon thyme and a sprinkle of paprika on each serving.

BOILED BEET GREENS AND CRISPY BACON

Boiled bacon and beet greens are a hearty side for fish, chicken, or beef. This recipe includes fresh lemon juice to help cut the slightly bitter taste of the beet leaves. Cook the leaves low and slow for a tender, flavorful dish that is loaded with nutrients.

YIELD: 4 servings

3 strips thick-cut bacon

Leaves from 4 large sugar beets

1 clove garlic, minced

½ teaspoon salt, divided

1 lemon, halved

¼ teaspoon ground pepper

¼ teaspoon sugar

Preheat the oven to 375°F.

Place the bacon in a 9-by-9-inch baking dish and bake until crispy, 30 to 40 minutes. Remove from the oven, drain the bacon on paper towels, and coarsely chop.

Clean the beet greens, leaving the stems. Fill a large saucepan three-fourths full with water. Over medium heat, bring the beet leaves, including the stems, to a boil. Add the garlic and ¼ teaspoon of the salt. Boil the leaves and stems until tender, about 2 minutes.

Remove the beet leaves and stems from the heat and immediately transfer them to a bowl of ice and water. When they are chilled completely through, transfer to a strainer. Pat the leaves and stems dry and place them on a serving platter.

Squeeze the juice from half of the lemon on the beet greens and stems. Sprinkle with the remaining ¼ teaspoon salt, pepper, and sugar. Top the beet greens and stems with the chopped bacon. Serve with lemon wedges cut from remaining lemon half.

CONSOMMÉ MADRILENE

Consommé Madrilene was trending on menus of the hotsy-totsy hotels where Scott and Zelda Fitzgerald lived in Manhattan. One of the most frequently ordered soups in the glamourous eateries, consommé Madrilene, is a tomato-based soup made with peppers, leeks, and chicken and beef broth. Steeped in the freshest flavors of the seasonal garden harvest, this light, flavorful soup is served chilled, making it the perfect lunch for a hot summer day.

You can serve it in soup bowls at lunch or dinner, or fill stemmed cordial glasses and pass a tray of the soup at a party.

YIELD: 12 servings

4 cups whole peeled canned tomatoes, undrained

4 cups beef broth

4 cups chicken broth

2 cups chopped carrots

1 cup chopped leeks

1 large Spanish or white onion, chopped

Juice of 1 lemon

½ cup chopped red bell pepper, plus more for garnish

1 clove garlic, minced

¼ teaspoon salt

1 teaspoon freshly ground multicolor peppercorns, divided

2 tablespoons chopped fresh cilantro

In a large saucepan over medium-high heat, add the tomatoes, beef broth, chicken broth, carrots, leeks, onion, lemon juice, bell pepper, garlic, salt, and ½ teaspoon of the ground pepper, and bring to a boil. Decrease the heat to medium and simmer with half of the lemon that was used for juicing for about 1 hour.

Remove from the heat and strain through a fine-mesh sieve into a large mixing bowl. Set in the refrigerator until chilled completely through, about 1 hour.

Serve in a soup bowl or in a hollowed-out half of a red bell pepper. Garnish with diced red bell pepper and fresh cilantro. Sprinkle with the remaining ½ teaspoon pepper.

MANHATTAN CLAM CHOWDER

▽

"For over a year he had been beating his way along the south shore of Lake Superior as a clam-digger..." —CHAPTER 6

Clam chowder—and clams prepared in all sorts of ways—would have been everywhere in the fictitious town of West Egg where Jay Gatsby lived and famously entertained. Clam chowder was one of the most popular soups of the 1920s. This recipe for Manhattan Island clam chowder combines creamy-based New England clam chowder with tomato-y Manhattan clam chowder to create the perfect soup for a Gatsby soirée.

For the best clam chowder, use fresh clams. Be careful to time it just right when they are added so the clams don't overcook.

YIELD: 6 servings

2 tablespoons butter

2 tablespoons extra-virgin olive oil

1 cup chopped red onion

½ cup chopped celery heart

1 tablespoon chopped
green bell pepper

1 clove garlic, minced

½ of a large russet potato,
peeled and diced

One 28-ounce can diced
tomatoes, undrained

12 ounces fresh or canned clams,
drained, rinsed, and chopped

1 teaspoon sea salt

½ teaspoon freshly
ground black pepper

½ teaspoon paprika

Juice of 1 lemon

½ cup chopped fresh
lemon thyme, divided

¼ cup chopped fresh chives

In a large saucepan over medium-high heat, melt the butter. Add the olive oil, onion, celery, bell pepper, and garlic. Sauté until softened, about 2 minutes. Add the potato, tomatoes, clams, salt, ground pepper, paprika, lemon juice, and ¼ cup of the lemon thyme. Bring to a boil and cook for 1 to 2 minutes, then decrease the heat to medium and cook until the potato pieces are tender, 30 to 40 minutes.

Serve in soup bowls, garnished with the remaining ¼ cup lemon thyme and the chives.

FROZEN TOMATO SALAD

In the jazz era, frozen salads were a delicious and refreshing way to celebrate the garden produce of the season. There was no air conditioning, so home cooks and chefs looked for ways to prepare foods that would help guests cool down. Anything cooling would help. The abundance of heirloom tomatoes in gardens made frozen tomato salad a popular treat.

Frozen salads were set in the icebox to freeze in molds that were also used for forming gelatin salads. Presented on a cake plate with colorful garnishes, a frozen salad could be the star of the table.

The salad will begin to melt in just a few minutes out of the freezer, so serve it immediately after presenting it. Only place a small amount on each salad plate so that it won't go over the edge if no one touches it and it melts completely.

YIELD: 10 to 12 servings

12 small vine-ripened tomatoes

2 teaspoons gelatin powder

1 tablespoon cold water

1 cup sour cream

½ cup chopped fresh chives

Juice of 1 large lemon

1 teaspoon Worcestershire sauce

½ teaspoon hot Hungarian paprika

1 large shallot, diced

1 clove garlic, minced

Cooking spray

8 grape or cherry tomatoes

Fresh curly parsley sprigs

12 iceberg lettuce leaves

SPECIALTY TOOLS

Gelatin mold (optional); or a parchment paper-lined 9-by-4-inch bread loaf pan

Peel and chop the vine-ripened tomatoes, cleaning and discarding the inner core of each one.

In a small bowl, dissolve the gelatin powder in the cold water.

In a blender, combine the chopped tomatoes, gelatin mixture, sour cream, chives, lemon juice, Worcestershire sauce, paprika, shallot, and garlic, and pulse until well combined.

Coat the inside of a gelatin salad mold with cooking spray. Pour the tomato mixture into the gelatin mold. Cover the mold with foil or plastic and set in the freezer for at least 3 hours.

Dip the mold in a large container of hot water for 1 to 2 seconds to release the tomato salad from the mold. Remove the covering. Place a plate over the top of the mold, and invert the salad onto the plate. Place the plate adjacent to a cake plate, and slide it onto the cake plate. Arrange the grape tomatoes on the top and parsley around the edge.

Serve a slice of the salad on an iceberg lettuce leaf on top of a salad plate.

PEACH SALAD

At the height of summer in the mid-1920s, peach salads were on almost every table in America. There were different ideas for how to fill a peach half in the recipe section of every newspaper. Some were filled with savory cream cheese spreads, and some with sweet fillings made with other fruits.

Peach salads are a delicious way to enjoy these wonderful stone fruits, and they can add a colorful, pretty presentation to any summer meal or party.

This recipe for a tangy cherry-filled peach salad is based on one that was shared in The Cincinnati Enquirer (Ohio) on July 17, 1925.

YIELD: 4 servings

4 large peaches

½ cup chopped mixed nuts

½ cup chopped maraschino cherries

1 cup mayonnaise

Fresh curly parsley sprigs

Pare and cut the peaches in half and remove the stones. Prepare two halves for each plate. In a medium mixing bowl, place the peach halves into ice water to chill and help prevent prevent turning brown.

In a small mixing bowl, mix together the nuts, cherries, and mayonnaise. Fill the space where the stone was with the nut and cherry filling.

Garnish with fresh curly parsley, and serve on a salad plate.

PINEAPPLE-LIME GELATIN SALAD

Increased availability of canned fruits and boxed gelatins transformed menus in the 1920s. Pretty gelatin salads added color and intrigue with the many different shapes of molds that became trendy. Gelatin salads could be shared in the shape of stars, hearts, flowers, and more and were the crown jewel of dining room tables everywhere. The salads were easily embellished by adding fruits from a wide array of options. Canned, crushed or cubed pineapple, raspberries, pear slices—even shredded fresh carrots—were popular options for creating crave-worthy delights that brought family and friends together. Whipped cream was folded in before letting the salad set overnight in the refrigerator, and some salads were topped with whipped cream. The salads were so satisfying that many people saved them for dessert.

Let this recipe be the star of your next party by making it in a star-shape mold. The vibrant green color, studded with crimson red cherries, makes this an ideal salad for the holidays.

YIELD: 10 to 12 servings

2½ cups water, divided

One 6-ounce package lime gelatin

One 8-ounce package
cream cheese, softened

One 8-ounce can crushed
pineapple, undrained

1 cup pineapple juice

½ of a 12-ounce jar
maraschino cherries

2 cups fresh whipped
cream, for garnish

1 teaspoon freshly grated
lime peel, for garnish

SPECIALTY TOOLS

8-cup gelatin mold (optional);
or a parchment paper-lined
9-by-4-inch bread loaf pan

In medium saucepan, bring 2 cups of the water to a boil. Pour the gelatin into a large bowl, add the boiling water, and stir until dissolved.

Add the cream cheese, and mix until it is blended completely.

Use a large spoon to stir in the crushed pineapple and pineapple juice, remaining ½ cup cold water, and the cherries. Reserve one cherry for garnish. Stir to blend all of the ingredients together well. Pour into the mold and refrigerate until set, 4 to 5 hours.

When the gelatin is set, place a serving plate over the mold and then invert the mold onto the plate. If the mold does not release the gelatin right away, dip the bottom of the mold into a large bowl of hot water for a few seconds. Jiggle until the mold releases the gelatin salad.

Garnish with piped whipped cream and lime zest, and place reserved cherry in the middle. Present on a pedastal cake plate, and serve on salad plates.

JULIA ARTHUR SALAD

In 1916 and 1917, newspapers across the United States published favorite recipes of some of the celebrated actors of the time. Popular actress Julia Arthur shared her favorite recipe. It was a combination of diced celery hearts, quartered heads of lettuce, sliced and seeded green grapes, and tangerine segments in a mayonnaise dressing. The Julia Arthur salad, as it was dubbed, quickly became so well-liked that the Biltmore Hotel in New York City, where Scott and Zelda Fitzgerald lived for a time, even put it on their lunch menus.

YIELD: 4 servings

SALAD

4 cups shredded iceberg lettuce

2 cups diced celery hearts

2 cups green grapes,
sliced lengthwise

1 cup mandarin orange segments

1 cup fresh lemon thyme leaves

DRESSING

1 cup mayonnaise

1 tablespoon apple cider vinegar

1 clove garlic, minced

1 tablespoon fresh
lemon thyme leaves

Juice and zest of 1 lemon

¼ teaspoon sugar

¼ teaspoon sea salt

¼ teaspoon ground pepper

To make the salad: Divide the lettuce among four salad plates. Place the remaining salad ingredients on top.

To make the dressing: Combine all of the ingredients in a salad shaker; stir and then shake well to combine. Drizzle over each salad.

ALLIGATOR PEAR SALAD

Alligator pear salad was on menus at many of the finest hotels in New York City around the time that F. Scott Fitzgerald lived there. Alligator pear is what avocados were called at the time. Newspapers in the 1920s were filled with recipes for alligator pear salads and instructions for how to get the avocado away from the peel.

One recipe, in The Evening Sun *(Baltimore, Maryland) on April 24, 1925, included pieces of orange with cubed avocado sprinkled with fresh lemon juice. The article recommended serving the salad in cocktail glasses for "a particularly delicious beginning for a dinner." Here is a similar recipe to the salad featured in the story.*

YIELD: 4 servings

SALAD

Leaves of 1 small head red cabbage

2 large avocados, peeled, pitted, and sliced

1 red bell pepper, seeded and diced

1 green bell pepper, seeded and diced

1 yellow bell pepper, seeded and diced

1 cup mandarin orange segments

½ cup chopped fresh chives

½ cup chopped fresh cilantro leaves

DRESSING

1 cup mayonnaise

1 tablespoon apple cider vinegar

1 clove garlic, minced

¼ cup fresh cilantro leaves

Juice and zest of 3 limes

¼ teaspoon sugar

¼ teaspoon sea salt

¼ teaspoon ground pepper

To make the salad: Divide the red cabbage leaves among four salad plates. Mix the remaining salad ingredients and divide them among the four salad plates.

To make the dressing: Combine all of the ingredients in a salad shaker; stir and then shake well to combine. Drizzle over each salad.

WALDORF SALAD

The Waldorf-Astoria was one of the most fashionable hotels in the world in the early 1920s. It was here that the Waldorf salad, one of the most classic American salads, was created. Hotel maître d' Oscar Tschirky is credited for developing the recipe for the Waldorf salad. He made the salad in March 1896 for a charity event at the hotel to benefit St. Mary's Hospital for Children. The first recipe was a mix of celery and apples pulled together with a simple dressing of lightly tangy mayonnaise. By the 1920s, walnuts were part of the salad, adding a whole new layer of flavor and crunch, similar to what we know today.

Waldorf salad can be served in a bowl, on individual salad plates, or in bite-size servings presented in small leaves of Belgian endive.

This recipe features hearts of celery, which are more tender, lighter, and crisper than the other parts of the celery stalk.

YIELD: 10 to 12 servings

3 large Honeycrisp apples with skins on, diced

1 cup finely sliced hearts of celery

1 cup lightly toasted chopped walnuts

1 cup green grapes, sliced lengthwise

2 cups mayonnaise

½ teaspoon pink sea salt

½ teaspoon freshly ground multicolor peppercorns

¼ teaspoon sugar

1 bunch oakleaf lettuce

2 medium heads Belgian endive

In a large mixing bowl, combine all of the ingredients except the lettuce and endive. Use a large spoon to lightly fold the ingredients together.

Arrange the oakleaf lettuce on a large serving platter, being careful to ensure that the platter is completely covered by the lettuce.

Pull the largest and strongest leaves from the heads of endive, and use a spoon to fill in the cavity of each leaf with about 1 tablespoon of the salad. Arrange the endive leaves on the lettuce leaves.

CRANBERRY FLUFF SALAD

Marshmallows were widely available by the 1920s. They were so popular that by 1927, the Girl Scouts Handbook *shared a recipe for a new treat called "Some More."*

In 1919, a marshmallow salad called cranberry fluff first appeared in newspapers. Louisa Grace won first place in a The Des Moines Tribune *recipe contest in January 1920 with her recipe for cranberry fluff, which she said her Finnish landlady had taught her about.*

This salad is sweet and fluffy with a bit of tartness from cranberries. Tiny bits of apple add sweetness. Slice the grapes and add them just before serving to help prevent them from browning around the edges. Fold in some chopped nuts for flavor and texture.

This salad is so pretty, it should be served in a clear glass serving bowl or in individual clear glasses so the bright, candy cane-pink color can brighten the table.

YIELD: 8 servings

2 cups frozen cranberries

1 cup mini marshmallows

⅓ cup sugar

¼ teaspoon sea salt

1 cup diced Honeycrisp apple

½ cup chopped walnuts

2 cups green grapes

1 cup whipped cream

Using a food processor, grind the cranberries. In a large bowl, combine the cranberries, marshmallows, sugar, and salt. Cover and refrigerate overnight.

Add the apple, walnuts, and grapes, and mix together well. Gently fold in the whipped cream.

MAIN COURSES

Gatsby's Spiced Baked Ham with Champagne Sauce 57
Salmon Loaf 58
Gatsby's Lemon-Roasted Turkey 60
Nick's Pig Sausages and Mashed Potatoes 61
Tom and Daisy's Cold Fried Chicken 63
Stuffed Brook Trout Véronique 64
Scott and Zelda's Pale Ale–Braised Pork Chops with Stewed Green Apples 67
Zelda's Garden Basil Mayo Tomato Sandwiches 68
Zelda's Applejack Omelet 69
Tom's "Celebrated" Sandwiches 71
Porterhouse Steak 71
Reuben 72
Fried Scallops 74
Nick's High-Tea Finger Sandwiches 75
Strawberry-Mint 75
Cilantro-Radish 77
Tarragon-Carrot 77
Garlicky Cucumber 78
Honey-Roasted Garden Beet Sandwiches 79

GATSBY'S SPICED BAKED HAM WITH CHAMPAGNE SAUCE

"…spiced baked hams crowded against salads of harlequin designs…" —CHAPTER 3

A spiced baked ham is a delicious centerpiece of any party. To put a Gatsby spin on a party ham, like the kind that Nick describes seeing, serve it with Champagne sauce, which was trending at the time. Ham with Champagne sauce was on the menus of fashionable hotels everywhere, and yet was so versatile that it was widely shared from one home cook to another in the pages of 1920s newspapers.

Drizzle the sauce generously over each slice of ham. This sauce is also wonderful with whitefish or pork.

YIELD: 10 to 12 servings

HAM

One 7- to 9-pound ham, uncut

One 20-ounce can pineapple rings, drained

12 maraschino cherries

1 cup brown sugar

1 cup Champagne

CHAMPAGNE SAUCE

1 teaspoon butter

1 teaspoon extra-virgin olive oil

1 shallot, minced

1 clove garlic, minced

1½ cups Champagne

1 cup heavy cream

1 tablespoon chopped fresh tarragon

½ teaspoon sea salt

¼ teaspoon freshly ground multicolor peppercorns

SPECIALTY TOOLS

Bamboo cocktail picks or toothpicks

To make the ham: Preheat the oven to 350°F.

Place the ham in the center of a roasting pan. Use bamboo picks or toothpicks to attach the pineapple rings all around the ham. Place a cherry in the center of each pineapple ring.

Make a slurry by mixing together the brown sugar and Champagne. Pour this over the ham.

Roast 12 to 15 minutes per pound.

To make the sauce: In a large saucepan over medium heat, melt the butter and heat the oil. Add the shallot and garlic, and sauté for 2 to 3 minutes. Add the remaining sauce ingredients. Bring to a boil, and boil until the sauce thickens, 20 to 30 minutes.

Remove from the heat, and provide to guests in a gravy boat as an option to drizzle on the ham.

SALMON LOAF

"...and a salmon-fisher or in any other capacity that
brought him food and bed." —CHAPTER 6

F. Scott Fitzgerald was known to snack on tinned meats. He wasn't alone. Tinned and canned meats were very popular in the 1920s. New recipes for salmon loaf made with canned salmon were shared in newspapers and featured on menus everywhere. Salmon loaf was a favorite meal in many households.

This salmon loaf includes fresh lemon juice for a citrusy zip. Fresh parsley and chives create a complex blend of flavors. Drizzle the creamy dill sauce over each piece and top with a sprig of fresh dill. Add fresh lemon to each plate for an extra spurt of flavor.

YIELD: 10 to 12 servings

Two 15-ounce cans salmon

1 cup crushed rich butter crackers

3 large eggs

½ cup milk

1 clove garlic, minced

Juice of ½ of a lemon

¼ cup chopped red onion

¼ cup chopped fresh dill

¼ cup chopped fresh parsley, plus more for garnish

¼ cup chopped fresh chives

1 teaspoon dried ground mustard

1 teaspoon paprika

Lemon wedges, for garnish

Fresh thyme sprig, for garnish

Preheat the oven to 375°F. Grease a loaf pan.

Using a strainer, rinse the salmon in cold water. Using your fingertips, go through the salmon very meticulously, picking out any bones or spines of the fish.

In a large mixing bowl, combine the salmon, crackers, eggs, milk, garlic, lemon juice, onion, dill, parsley, chives, mustard, and paprika. Use your hands to mix the ingredients together very well, 3 to 4 minutes. The mixture will be very wet, and will become drier as it is mixed. The wetter the mixture, the moister the salmon loaf will be after it bakes.

Place the mixture in the prepared loaf pan, and bake until it is golden brown and cooked all the way through, 35 to 40 minutes.

Garnish with lemon wedges, parsley, and fresh thyme sprig.

GATSBY'S LEMON-ROASTED TURKEY

"...turkeys bewitched to a dark gold..." —CHAPTER 3

The very best whole roast turkey is lightly stuffed with cut fresh lemons. Keep them in the whole time. Place thin slices of fresh lemon between the skin and breast meat. Create a flavorful basting liquid by adding pinot grigio, salt and pepper, and some sliced onions to the roasting pan. Fresh thyme and tarragon add flavor as well.

Serve the turkey sliced, with bread and condiments placed alongside for the option of making a sandwich.

YIELD: 12 to 15 servings

One 15-pound turkey

3 large lemons, sliced

3 large red onions, cut into quarters, divided

2 cups chopped fresh tarragon

1 cup chopped fresh thyme

2 cups pinot grigio

1 teaspoon salt

1 teaspoon pepper

2 tablespoons butter

If the turkey is frozen, thaw it in the refrigerator for 3 days.

Plan enough time to roast a turkey for 13 minutes per pound of turkey.

Preheat the oven to 350°F.

Clean the turkey by rinsing it all over in cold water in the sink. Remove the neck and the bag of turkey parts.

Grease a roasting pan. Place the lemon slices, 4 of the onion quarters, and the tarragon and thyme in the cavity and under the skin of the turkey. Place the turkey in the prepared pan and pour the wine over, then season with the salt and pepper. Cut the butter into three pats of equal size, and place one pat under the skin and two pats on top of the turkey. Arrange the remaining onion quarters around the turkey.

Place the turkey in the oven. After the first 90 minutes, pull the turkey and use a baster or a spoon to baste it with the wine-and-butter mixture. Put the turkey back in the oven. Repeat the basting step after about another hour. Make sure to cover the whole turkey as much as possible.

According to U.S. Department of Agriculture safety guidance, the turkey must reach 165°F before it is safe to eat. Use a meat thermometer to check the temperature.

When the turkey is done, remove it from the oven and set it aside for approximately 10 minutes until the heat is reduced enough to touch. Place the turkey on a large platter to present it whole, cutting it for party guests according to the type of meat that each guest prefers.

NICK'S PIG SAUSAGES AND MASHED POTATOES

"I knew the other clerks and young bond-salesmen by their first names, and lunched with them in dark, crowded restaurants on little pig sausages and mashed potatoes and coffee. I even had a short affair with a girl who lived in Jersey City and worked in the accounting department, but her brother began throwing mean looks in my direction, so when she went on her vacation in July,
I let it blow quietly away." —CHAPTER 3

To serve this as a party appetizer, place ½ cup of the potatoes in a cocktail glass, and top the potatoes with bite-size pieces of sausage and a sprinkle of fresh parsley.

YIELD: 4 servings

SAUSAGES

1 tablespoon butter

1 tablespoon extra-virgin olive oil

1 pound Polish sausage, sliced ½ inch thick

1 large red bell pepper

1 large green bell pepper

1 large yellow bell pepper

1 large red onion

1 large fennel bulb and fronds, finely sliced

1 clove garlic, minced

½ teaspoon sea salt

½ teaspoon freshly ground black pepper

POTATOES

4 large russet potatoes, peeled

¾ cup milk

2 tablespoons butter

1 clove garlic, minced

½ teaspoon salt

¼ teaspoon freshly ground black pepper

To make the sausages: In a large skillet over medium-high heat, melt the butter and heat the oil. Add the slices and heat them in the skillet.

To cut the bell peppers: Use a knife to slice about ½ inch of the bottoms and tops off of each of the peppers. Slice each pepper lengthwise in the spaces between where the veins connect with the flesh. Discard the veins and seeds. Cut each section into quarters.

To cut the onion: Use a knife to slice off ½ inch of the top of the onion. Without cutting all the way through, slice the onion lengthwise 4 to 6 times, depending on the size of the onion. Turn the onion and cut the same amount of slices in the other direction. Lay the onion on its side and cut ¼-inch-thick slices to dice the onion.

When the sausages are halfway through cooking, about 15 minutes, add the vegetables and seasonings. Reserve a bit of the fennel fronds to use as a garnish when serving. Sauté the ingredients together until the vegetables are translucent and the meat is no longer pink inside, about 30 minutes. Stir occasionally with a spatula.

To make the potatoes: Bring a large saucepan of salted water to a boil over high heat. Add the potatoes and cook until a fork easily pierces all the way through, 25 to 30 minutes. Remove the saucepan from the heat and drain the water.

Using a potato masher, mash the potatoes in the pan with the milk, butter, garlic, salt, and pepper until smooth. To serve, place the potatoes on a plate and top them with the sausages and vegetables.

TOM AND DAISY'S COLD FRIED CHICKEN

"Daisy and Tom were sitting opposite each other at the kitchen table,
with a plate of cold fried chicken between them, and two bottles of
ale. He was talking intently across the table at her, and in his earnestness
his hand had fallen upon and covered her own. Once in a while she
looked up at him and nodded in agreement.
They weren't happy, and neither of them had touched the chicken or the
ale—and yet they weren't unhappy either. There was an unmistakable air of
natural intimacy about the picture, and anybody would have said that they
were conspiring together." —CHAPTER 7

Few foods are better on a hot summer day than cold fried chicken. Leftovers taste the best. This recipe for fried chicken can be made on a Sunday and kept in the refrigerator for a weekday picnic—with two bottles of ale.

YIELD: 6 to 8 servings

1 quart vegetable oil

2 cups all-purpose flour

1 tablespoon paprika

1½ teaspoons sea salt

1 teaspoon freshly ground
black peppercorns

½ cup buttermilk

2 eggs

3 tablespoons lemon juice

4 pounds fryer chicken,
cut into pieces

In a Dutch oven over medium-high heat, bring the oil to 375°F.

In a large mixing bowl, combine the flour, paprika, salt, and pepper, and stir with a spoon to blend together well.

In a separate bowl, whisk together the buttermilk, eggs, and lemon juice.

Dip each piece of the chicken in the milk mixture, and cover it well. Then coat it in the dry ingredients.

Fry the chicken, 3 or 4 pieces at a time, until golden brown, 8 to 12 minutes on each side per piece.

STUFFED BROOK TROUT VÉRONIQUE

▼

Stuffed brook trout with Véronique sauce was on menus of some of the finest hotels in New York City in the 1920s. It appeared occasionally on the menus of the Biltmore Hotel in New York City around the time that Scott and Zelda Fitzgerald stayed there for an extended time.

Véronique sauce is a rich, creamy, lemony sauce—like Hollandaise sauce—that is made with fresh tarragon and white grapes.

Serve this on a platter on a buffet, or plate the fish and sauce in individual servings to pass around or set out on a table at a party. Accentuate the unusualness of the grapes as an ingredient for fish by garnishing the fish with tender grape leaves from the garden or bits of fresh tarragon sprinkled around.

YIELD: 4 servings

STUFFING

1 tablespoon butter

1 tablespoon extra-virgin olive oil

2 cups scallops

1 large red bell pepper, seeded and diced

1 clove garlic, minced

Juice of 1 lemon

¼ teaspoon sea salt

¼ teaspoon ground pepper

½ cup crushed rich butter crackers

FISH

2 whole small trout or other whitefish

1 tablespoon butter

VÉRONIQUE SAUCE

1 pint heavy cream

2 tablespoons dry vermouth

Juice of ½ lemon

20 grapes

1 cup fresh tarragon, chopped

Lemon wedges, for garnish

1 cup fresh dill, for garnish

Preheat the oven to 375°F.

To make the stuffing: In a large skillet over medium-high heat, melt the butter and heat the oil. Add the scallops, red bell pepper, garlic, lemon juice, salt, and ground pepper, and sauté until the scallops are firm and cooked all the way through, about 20 minutes.

In a large mixing bowl, combine the scallop mixture with the crushed crackers, using your hands to mix the ingredients together lightly.

To make the fish: Fill the inside of each fish with the stuffing. Use metal skewers to poke through the skin on the top and bottom to secure the stuffing in the fish while it bakes, or prop the fish up against each other well to secure them in the baking dish.

Grease a 9-inch round baking dish or roasting pan with the butter, place the fish in the pan, and bake until the fish flakes easily with a fork and the stuffing is cooked all the way through, about 30 minutes.

To make the Véronique sauce: In a large skillet over medium-high heat, combine the cream, vermouth, and lemon juice, and bring to a boil. Boil until the mixture thickens, 15 to 20 minutes.

Peel and slice the grapes lengthwise. To easily peel grapes, set them in some boiling water for 1 to 2 seconds. Use your fingers to carefully find where the peel meets, and pull away to separate the peel from the grape. Add the grapes and tarragon to the sauce, and simmer for about 10 minutes.

Serve the sauce over the fish. Garnish with lemon wedges and fresh dill.

SCOTT AND ZELDA'S PALE ALE–BRAISED PORK CHOPS WITH STEWED GREEN APPLES

In a love letter to Scott in 1930, Zelda reminded him of their time in New York City. Zelda wrote: "We Drank Bass pale ale. We drank always."

Simmer these pork chops, low and slow, in rich pale ale.

YIELD: 4 servings

PORK CHOPS

4 bone-in pork chops, about ¾ inch thick

Two 12-ounce cans pale ale, divided

1 cup packed brown sugar

3 teaspoons chopped fresh rosemary, divided

1 tablespoon paprika

½ teaspoon sea salt

½ teaspoon freshly ground multicolor peppercorns

1 tablespoon butter

1 tablespoon extra-virgin olive oil

STEWED GREEN APPLES

6 large green apples with skins on, cored and sliced thin, unpeeled

1 vanilla bean

½ teaspoon freshly grated nutmeg

1 cup brown sugar

Juice of 2 lemons

1 cinnamon stick

½ teaspoon allspice

½ teaspoon ground cinnamon

SPECIALTY TOOLS

Nutmeg grater

Preheat the oven to 350°F.

To make the pork chops: Set the pork chops in a 9-by-12-inch cake pan or marinating container, and pour one can of the pale ale over them. Seal the container and place in the refrigerator for at least 2 hours or overnight. Discard the marinade.

Rinse the pork chops in cold water, and pat them dry with paper towels.

In a large mixing bowl, combine the brown sugar, 2 teaspoons of the rosemary, the paprika, salt, and pepper. Stir the ingredients to blend them well. Toss the pork chops, one at a time, in the mixture until each chop is well coated all over.

In a frying pan over medium-high heat, melt the butter and heat the oil. Add the pork chops and sear the exterior by browning them on both sides, about 2 to 3 minutes on each side.

Remove the pork chops from the frying pan and arrange them in a Dutch oven. Pour ½ can of pale ale over them. Pour the sauce from the frying pan over them. Bake until they are cooked all the way through and the inside is white, 40 to 45 minutes. Each pork chop should have an internal temperature of 145°F. When the pork chops are done, remove them from the oven and set them on the countertop until they are cool enough to plate.

To make the stewed green apples: Place the apples in a Dutch oven over high heat. Using a knife, cut the vanilla bean open and scrape it once, lengthwise, to pull away the vanilla seeds. Add the vanilla bean and seeds, nutmeg, brown sugar, lemon juice, cinnamon stick, allspice, and ground cinnamon. Bring to a boil, and then reduce the heat to medium. Simmer, stirring occasionally, until the apples are saucy and chunky, about 40 minutes. Remove the cinnamon stick and vanilla bean pod.

Plate the pork chops and stewed green apples. Garnish with the remaining 1 teaspoon rosemary.

ZELDA'S GARDEN BASIL MAYO TOMATO SANDWICHES

"I hope they'll have tomato sandwiches at lunch," said Zelda. "I adore tomato sandwiches and lemonade. It's all I ate in Alabama." —ZELDA FITZGERALD, *CALL ME ZELDA*

These tomato sandwiches are best made at the peak of summer when the garden is overflowing with plump, soft, orange–ruby red tomatoes. Heirlooms make the best sandwiches. They are the kind that Zelda Fitzgerald would have loved on a warm day.

These sandwiches are embellished with mayonnaise accented with garden-fresh basil. Use a food processor to combine the ingredients and to release the flavor of the basil.

YIELD: 4 servings

4 large heirloom tomatoes, thinly sliced

1 cup mayonnaise

Juice of ½ lemon

½ cup chiffonade fresh basil, plus more for garnish

½ teaspoon sea salt, divided

½ teaspoon freshly ground black pepper, divided

8 slices bread

Lemon wedges, for serving

Place the tomato slices on a plate lined with paper towels to dry them. Set them aside.

While the tomatoes are drying, make the basil mayo. In a food processor, combine the mayonnaise, lemon juice, basil, and ¼ teaspoon each of the salt and pepper. Pulse to blend well.

Toast the bread slices.

Spread the basil mayonnaise on half of the bread slices. Arrange the tomato slices on top of the basil mayo. Sprinkle the remaining ¼ teaspoon salt and ¼ teaspoon pepper on top of the tomato slices. Place a bread slice on top of the tomatoes. Cut each sandwich diagonally, and garnish with lemon wedges and additional basil.

ZELDA'S APPLEJACK OMELET

"I fell in love with her courage, her sincerity, and her flaming self-respect."

—F. SCOTT FITZGERALD, IN A LETTER TO HIS AND ZELDA'S ONLY CHILD, SCOTTIE

While visiting Fitzgerald's alma mater, Princeton, Zelda turned cartwheels down Prospect Street and showed up for breakfast waving a bottle of applejack, requesting "omelet flambé."

YIELD: 6 servings

SAUCE

2 large apples

2 cups applejack brandy
or any brandy

6 ounces thick-cut bacon

1 pint heavy cream

Juice of 1 lemon

¼ teaspoon sea salt

¼ teaspoon freshly
ground black pepper

TOASTED WALNUTS

½ cup walnuts

1 teaspoon brown sugar

1 teaspoon extra-virgin olive oil

EGGS

1 tablespoon butter

1 tablespoon extra-virgin olive oil

10 large eggs

½ cup club soda

¼ teaspoon sea salt

¼ teaspoon freshly
ground black pepper

1 cup grated Cheddar cheese

To make the sauce: Prepare the sauce 2 hours ahead. Core and cut the apples into very thin slices (do not peel). In a medium mixing bowl, add the apples and brandy. Cover with plastic wrap and chill in the refrigerator for 2 hours or up to 8 hours.

Preheat the oven to 350°F.

Place the bacon in a baking dish and bake until crispy and browned, 20 to 30 minutes.

When the bacon is cool enough to handle, use tongs to set it on a plate lined with paper towels, and pat the bacon to remove the grease. Chop the bacon into a small dice.

In a large frying pan over high heat, combine the cream, lemon juice, salt, and pepper. Bring the sauce to a boil. Cook, stirring occasionally, until the sauce thickens, 20 to 30 minutes. Add the apples, and stir the brandy and bacon into the sauce during the last 10 minutes.

To make the toasted walnuts: In a small mixing bowl, toss the walnuts in the brown sugar and oil. Spread in a small baking dish and roast until lightly browned on the outside, 8 to 10 minutes. Watch them very closely to make sure they do not burn. Set a timer as a reminder. Remove from the oven, transfer to a plate, and let cool.

To make the eggs: In a large frying pan over medium-high heat, melt the butter and heat the oil.

In a medium bowl, whisk together the eggs, club soda, salt, and pepper until well combined. Pour half of the egg mixture into the frying pan and cook the eggs until they are brown on the bottom, then use a spatula to flip the eggs to brown the other side, about 10 minutes. Flip one side over to the other side; repeat this to fold the eggs over twice. Transfer to a plate. Make a second omelet with the remaining egg mixture.

Top each omelet with the sauce, making sure to divide the apples and bacon evenly. Top with the toasted walnuts and sprinkle with the cheese.

TOM'S "CELEBRATED" SANDWICHES

"Tom rang for the janitor and sent him for some celebrated sandwiches,
which were a complete supper in themselves. I wanted to get out and walk
southward toward the park through the soft twilight, but each time I tried to go I
became entangled in some wild, strident argument which pulled me back, as if
with ropes, into my chair." —CHAPTER 2

*The "celebrated" sandwiches that Tom ordered might have included Swiss cheese melted over spiced and corned
beef brisket piled high under roasted sauerkraut and onions on dark rye bread; porterhouse steak filets smothered
in horseradish mayonnaise and stacked on marble rye bread; and rich, lightly breaded fried scallops packed inside
a sandwich bun with lemony mayonnaise. Variations of these were popular throughout the jazz age and are still
favorites today.*

PORTERHOUSE STEAK

YIELD: 4 servings

STEAKS

Four 8-ounce porterhouse
steaks, bone-in

¼ teaspoon salt

¼ teaspoon freshly
ground black pepper

1 tablespoon butter

1 tablespoon extra-virgin olive oil

HORSERADISH MAYONNAISE

1 cup mayonnaise

1 tablespoon coarsely
grated fresh horseradish

½ teaspoon fresh lemon juice

4 sandwich buns

To make the steaks: Sprinkle the steaks on both sides with the salt
and pepper.

In a large pan over medium-high heat, melt the butter and heat the
olive oil. Add the steaks and cook for 8 to 10 minutes on each side.
(You may need to do this in batches.)

When the steaks are done cooking, set them on a cutting board on the
countertop until they are cool enough to cut. Use a knife to cut the meat
from the bone and trim away the fat.

To make the horseradish mayonnaise: In a bowl, mix together the
mayonnaise, horseradish, and lemon juice until well blended.

Spread about 1 tablespoon mayonnaise on the bottoms of each bun.
Top each bottom bun with one-fourth of the meat. Top each with about
1 tablespoon of the remaining mayonnaise, then add top buns.

REUBEN

A fresh cut of corned beef brisket can be challenging to find at even the best butcher shops after St. Patrick's Day. Corned beef can taste even better, though, when it is made from scratch. Corned beef is made using beef brisket, which is available in most meat markets. Prepare the brine 6 days ahead.

YIELD: 4 servings

CORNED BEEF

12 cups water

¼ cup pickling spices

1 tablespoon whole cloves

1 tablespoon juniper berries

Juice of 1 large lemon

1 clove garlic, roughly chopped

¼ teaspoon sea salt

¼ teaspoon freshly ground black pepper

4 dried bay leaves

1 cup packed light brown sugar

2 pounds beef brisket

One 14-ounce package sauerkraut

1 cup sliced red onion

THOUSAND ISLAND DRESSING

1 cup mayonnaise

½ cup ketchup

1 tablespoon pickle relish

8 slices marble rye or pumpernickel bread

1 cup very thinly sliced red onion

To make the corned beef: Six days in advance, in a Dutch oven, add the water, pickling spices, cloves, juniper berries, lemon juice, garlic, salt, pepper, bay leaves, and brown sugar. Stir to dissolve the sugar and spices. Add the beef and turn to coat. Cover and place in the refrigerator. Turn the meat once each day for 6 days to ensure that all of the meat is evenly exposed to the brine. Remove the beef from the Dutch oven and discard the brine.

Preheat the oven to 325°F.

Rinse and drain the sauerkraut and spread it on the bottom of the Dutch oven. Spread the onion slices on top of the sauerkraut. Place the meat, fat side up, on top. Roast the beef in the oven until it falls apart with the touch of a fork, about 4 hours.

Remove the beef from the oven and set it on the countertop until it is cool enough to slice, then cut it into thin slices.

To make the dressing: Place the mayonnaise, ketchup, and relish in a large mixing bowl, and use a spoon to mix them together well.

Toast the bread. Spread each slice of bread with Thousand Island dressing.

Divide the sauerkraut among 4 of the bread slices. Arrange the meat on top of the sauerkraut. Place a small amount of red onion on top. Place a piece of bread on top of each sandwich. Slice diagonally.

FRIED SCALLOPS

YIELD: 4 servings

SCALLOPS

1 pound frozen scallops

Juice of 1 large lemon

6 tablespoons extra-virgin oil, for frying

1½ cups all-purpose flour

1 teaspoon pink Himalayan sea salt

½ teaspoon black pepper

1 tablespoon hot Hungarian paprika

1 large egg, lightly beaten

1½ cups beer

TARTAR SAUCE

2 cups mayonnaise

½ cup pickle relish

¼ teaspoon mustard seeds

¼ teaspoon sea salt

¼ teaspoon freshly ground black pepper

1 teaspoon fresh lemon juice

ASSEMBLY

4 sandwich buns

2 cups shredded iceberg lettuce

4 thin slices beefsteak tomato

Lemon wedges, for garnish

To make the scallops: Defrost the scallops in the refrigerator overnight or for at least 12 hours. Rinse them in cold water and drain them. Place them in a bowl with the lemon juice, toss to coat, and return them to the refrigerator until it is time to fry them.

In a large frying pan over medium-high heat, heat the oil.

In a medium mixing bowl, combine the flour, salt, pepper, paprika, egg, and beer, and mix well.

Toss the scallops in the breading, ensuring that they are coated evenly all over, and place them in the frying pan. Fry the scallops on each side until golden brown, 4 to 5 minutes on each side. Some of the coating may come off while the scallops are frying, and this is okay.

Use your index finger and thumb to feel a scallop to tell whether it is thoroughly cooked through. It should feel firm and tender, but not tough. The inside should not be pink.

To make the tartar sauce: In a small mixing bowl, combine all of the ingredients until well mixed.

To assemble the sandwiches: Place one-fourth of the scallops on the bottom of each of the sandwich buns. Top with the lettuce, tomato, and tartar sauce. Place the bun top on each sandwich and serve with lemon wedges.

NICK'S HIGH-TEA FINGER SANDWICHES

"'Nobody's coming to tea. It's too late!' He looked at his watch as if there was some pressing demand on his time elsewhere. 'I can't wait all day.'"

This assortment of five lovely finger sandwiches is inspired by the tiny two-bite nibbles that Daisy and Jay Gatsby enjoyed at their clandestine afternoon tea at Nick's cottage.

STRAWBERRY-MINT

YIELD: 6 servings

8 ounces cream cheese, softened

Juice of ½ lemon

1 teaspoon sugar

1 teaspoon salt

1 cup chopped fresh mint leaves

2 cups sliced strawberries

12 slices white bread

SPECIALTY TOOLS

Large scallop-edge
flower-shape cookie cutter.

In a stand mixer or in a bowl with a handheld mixer, beat the cream cheese, lemon juice, sugar, and salt on medium-high speed until well combined, 3 to 5 minutes. Add the mint and strawberries, reserving a bit of each for garnish, and blend again on medium speed.

Use a large, scallop-edge flower-shape cookie cutter to cut out the center of each slice of bread. Use a butter knife to spread the cream cheese mixture across half of the flowers. Ensure that all of the bread is covered.

Top each of the sandwiches with a bread flower slice, and secure each sandwich with a toothpick or a bamboo cocktail pick with a small strawberry and a few small mint leaves.

CILANTRO-RADISH

YIELD: 20 servings

8 to 10 small radishes

½ cup sour cream

½ cup chopped fresh
cilantro, divided

1 teaspoon crushed coriander
seeds (optional)

½ teaspoon fresh lemon juice

¼ teaspoon sea salt

¼ teaspoon freshly ground
black pepper, divided

¼ teaspoon sugar

10 slices whole wheat bread

Use a paring knife to slice the radishes into paper-thin slices.

In a stand mixer or in a bowl using a handheld mixer, combine the sour cream, two-thirds of the cilantro, the coriander seeds (if using), lemon juice, salt, ⅛ teaspoon of the pepper, and the sugar.

Use a knife to remove the crusts from the bread slices. Cut each slice of bread into 2 triangles. Use a butter knife to spread the sour cream mixture on half of the triangles. Place 2 or 3 radish slices on each triangle.

Place the remaining bread triangles on top. Sprinkle the remaining cilantro and pepper on top.

TARRAGON-CARROT

YIELD: 8 servings

3 large carrots

2 tablespoons chopped
fresh tarragon, divided

APPLE CIDER VINEGAR DRESSING

3 tablespoons apple cider vinegar

1 teaspoon extra-virgin olive oil

¼ teaspoon sea salt

¼ teaspoon freshly
ground black pepper

CREAM CHEESE SPREAD

4 ounces cream cheese, softened

¼ teaspoon sugar

8 slices white bread

Trim and peel the carrots. Using a peeler, shave the carrots into strips. Place in a bowl and add the tarragon.

To make the dressing: In a salad shaker, combine the apple cider vinegar, olive oil, salt, and pepper. Shake until all of the ingredients are well combined. Pour over the carrots and tarragon, and toss to coat.

To make the cream cheese spread: In a stand mixer or in a bowl using a handheld mixer, combine the cream cheese and sugar.

Use a knife to remove the crusts from the bread slices. Cut the bread slices into rectangles. Spread the cream cheese mixture on half of the rectangles.

Place 1 tablespoon of carrot-and-tarragon sandwich filling on top of the cream cheese mixture. Top each sandwich with one of the remaining rectangles. Place a toothpick or bamboo cocktail pick in the center of each sandwich to secure it.

Scatter the remaining ⅔ cup of tarragon on the sandwiches for garnish.

Opposite page:
Tarragon-Carrot (top tier back)
Cilantro-Radish (top tier left)
Garlicky Cucumber (top tier right)

GARLICKY CUCUMBER

"Cucumber sandwiches are a good, clean meal. I like clean foods. Clean people." —ZELDA FITZGERALD, *CALL ME ZELDA*

YIELD: 6 to 8 servings

1 cup plain yogurt

4 ounces cream cheese, softened

1 clove garlic, minced

Zest and juice of 1 lemon, divided

¼ teaspoon sea salt

¼ teaspoon freshly ground black peppercorns, divided

¼ teaspoon sugar

1 English cucumber (Use a regular cucumber if English cucumbers are not available; English cucumbers have less water content.)

10 slices whole wheat bread

SPECIALTY TOOLS

3-inch round cookie cutter, pastry bag, and ½-inch star frosting tip (optional; can also use a knife to cut sandwiches into squares or rectangles.)

In a stand mixer or in a bowl using a handheld mixer, combine the yogurt, cream cheese, garlic, 1 teaspoon of fresh lemon zest, the lemon juice, salt, ⅛ teaspoon of the pepper, and the sugar.

Slice the cucumber into ¼-inch slices.

Use the cookie cutter to cut circles out of the bread slices. Place three cucumber slices on each of the bread circles.

Fill a pastry bag fitted with a star tip by rolling down the sides all around and putting the cream cheese mixture in the bag with a large spoon. Pipe the cream cheese mixture on top of each of the cucumber slices.

Use a grater to zest the rind of the remaining lemon, and sprinkle lemon zest on top of each sandwich. Sprinkle the remaining ⅛ teaspoon pepper on top of the sandwiches.

HONEY-ROASTED GARDEN BEET SANDWICHES

YIELD: 8 servings

HONEY-ROASTED BEETS

2 large beets

2 tablespoons extra-virgin olive oil

1 tablespoon honey

1 clove garlic, minced

¼ teaspoon sea salt

¼ teaspoon freshly ground
multicolor peppercorns

APRICOT CHEESE SPREAD

8 ounces cream cheese, softened

½ cup apricot jam or jelly

3 tablespoons mayonnaise

¼ teaspoon sea salt

½ teaspoon freshly
ground black pepper

½ teaspoon paprika

ASSEMBLY

8 slices brioche bread or
other favorite bread

Oakleaf lettuce leaves

To make the honey-roasted beets: Preheat the oven to 350°F. Line a baking sheet with parchment paper.

Clean and trim the beets, discarding the ends. Use a knife to cut the beets lengthwise into ¼-inch-thick slices.

In a medium mixing bowl, combine the oil, honey, garlic, salt, and pepper, and blend well. Add the beets to the bowl and toss to coat.

Arrange the beets in a single layer on the prepared baking sheet. Roast until a fork easily pierces them all the way through, 30 to 40 minutes.

Remove the beets from the oven and set them on the countertop to cool.

To make the apricot cheese spread: Add all the ingredients to a food processor and blend until thoroughly combined. Transfer to a bowl, cover with plastic wrap, and chill in refrigerator for at least 16 hours or up to 24 hours so that the flavors can blend.

To assemble the sandwiches: Spread the cream cheese mixture on half of the bread slices. Place the beets on top of the cream cheese mixture, followed by the lettuce and the remaining bread slices. Cut each sandwich diagonally to make triangles.

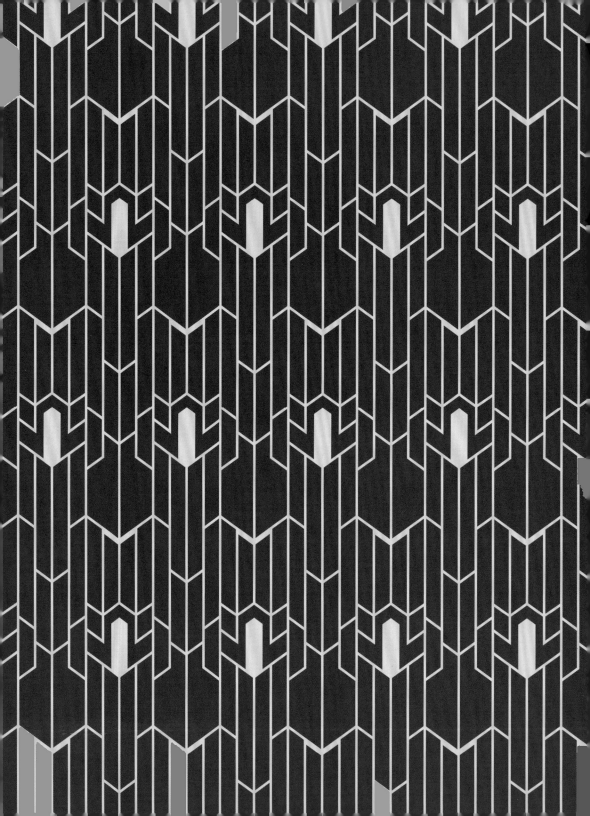

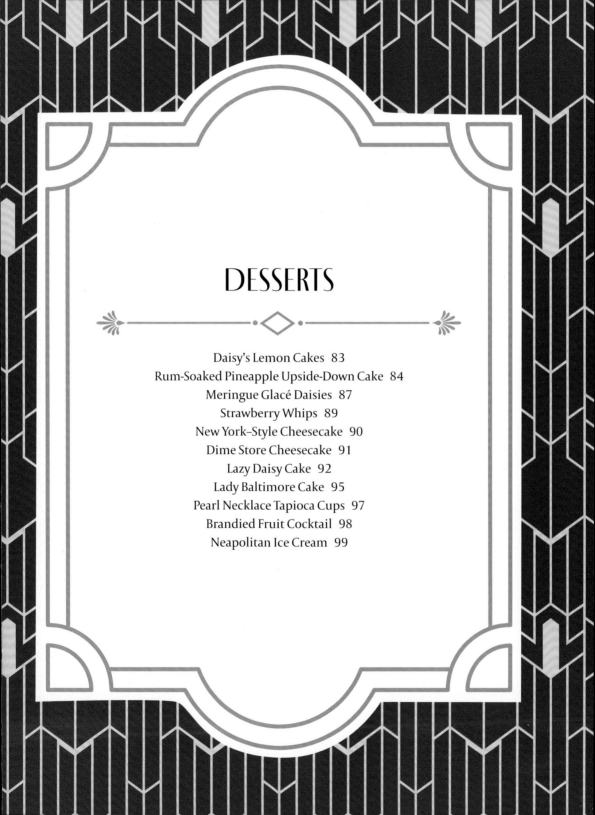

DESSERTS

DAISY'S LEMON CAKES

"'Have you got everything you need in the shape of—of tea?' I took him into the pantry, where he looked a little reproachfully at the Finn. Together we scrutinized the twelve lemon cakes from the delicatessen shop. 'Will they do?' I asked. 'Of course, of course! They're fine!' and he added hollowly, '... old sport.'" —CHAPTER 5

These lemon cakes are like the recipe that the Ritz Carlton Hotel made for tea in the 1920s.

Bake the cake in twelve small cake pans to make the lemon cakes the way that Nick bought them from the delicatessen for Jay Gatsby's high tea with Daisy Buchanan or bake all the batter a little longer in a Bundt pan for one large cake.

On October 8, 1928, a reader shared this recipe in The Daily Kennebec Journal *(Maine).*

"Lemon Cake: Five cups of flour white and clean; One cup of butter nothing mean. Six new laid eggs well buttered up. Enough of milk to fill one cup. One lemon large; two if small. Sugar three cups to sweeten all. Teaspoon of soda add, rich lemon cake will then be had. Bake it in pans to please the eye, round or oblong, should you try. Then one thing note without surprise: the more you make the less the size."

YIELD: 12 servings

CAKE

Cooking spray or melted butter

1 cup butter, room temperature, softened

3 cups granulated sugar

8 eggs

Juice of 1 large or 2 small lemons

1¾ cups whole milk

5 cups all-purpose flour

1 teaspoon baking soda

GLAZE

2 cups powdered sugar

2 tablespoons whole milk

GARNISH

1 cup edible flowers (violets, nasturtiums, etc.); and
½ cup fresh mint leaves

To make the cake: Preheat the oven to 350°F. Coat twelve 4-inch-round cake pans with cooking spray.

In the bowl of a stand mixer or in a bowl using a handheld mixer on high speed, cream the butter and sugar until light and fluffy. Add the eggs, one at a time, beating after each addition. Combine the lemon juice and milk. Combine the flour and baking soda. Alternately add flour and milk mixture to the egg mixture.

Pour the batter into the prepared pans until two-thirds full. Bake until a toothpick inserted into the center comes out clean, 35 to 40 minutes. Remove the cakes from the pans, and set on a rack to cool. Trim the tops level. Invert (bottoms up) to glaze.

To make the glaze: In a medium mixing bowl, stir together the powdered sugar and milk until it reaches a smooth consistency. If it is too watery, add more powdered sugar. Pour the glaze over the top of the cakes, using an offset spatula or butter knife to carefully and lightly guide the glaze all around.

Garnish the cakes with edible flowers and fresh mint leaves.

RUM-SOAKED PINEAPPLE UPSIDE-DOWN CAKE

▽

"At 158th Street the cab stopped at one slice in a long white
cake of apartment-houses." —CHAPTER 2

In 1925, out of more than 60,000 recipes submitted to the Hawaiian Pineapple Company's contest, 2,500 were for pineapple upside-down cake. In 1926, the book Pineapple as 100 Good Cooks Serve It *featured the recipe for pineapple upside-down cake that Mrs. Robert Davis of Norfolk, Virginia, submitted in the contest.*

YIELD: 6 servings

CAKE

Cooking spray or melted butter

1 whole pineapple

3 cups light rum

6 large pitted cherries

1 cup brandy

¾ cup butter, softened, divided

1 cup granulated sugar

3 small eggs

1 teaspoon vanilla extract

1½ cups all-purpose flour

1½ teaspoons baking powder

¼ teaspoon sea salt

⅔ cup light brown sugar

½ cup chopped walnuts

CREAM

1 pint heavy cream

1 tablespoon granulated sugar

SPECIALTY TOOLS

1¼-inch round cookie cutter

Maraschino cherries, for garnish

To make the cake: Preheat the oven to 350°F. Coat a 9-by-12-inch cake pan with cooking spray.

Cut the top and bottom off of the pineapple and cut away the peel. Slice the pineapple, widthwise, into seven ½-inch slices. Use a 1¼-inch round cookie cutter to cut a hole in the center of each pineapple slice. Place the pineapple slices in a large mixing bowl with the rum. Cover with plastic and set the bowl in the refrigerator for at least 2 hours or up to overnight. Drain the pineapple and pat dry with paper towels. Discard the rum.

Place the cherries in a small bowl with the brandy. Cover with plastic and set the bowl in the refrigerator for 6 to 8 hours. Drain the cherries and pat dry with paper towels. Discard the brandy.

In the bowl of a stand mixer or in a bowl using a handheld mixer on high speed, cream ½ cup of the butter with the granulated sugar until light and fluffy. Add the eggs, one at a time, mixing after each addition. Add the vanilla, and beat to combine.

In a medium bowl, add the flour, baking powder, and salt. Mix until well combined. Add to the butter and sugar mixture, and beat until the batter is smooth with no lumps.

In a small bowl, combine the remaining ¼ cup butter with the brown sugar. Use a fork to mix together until all of the brown sugar is moistened. Spread this on the bottom of the prepared cake pan.

Sprinkle the walnuts over the brown sugar, carefully making sure that the nuts are evenly distributed throughout the cake pan.

Arrange 6 pineapple slices in the brown sugar mixture in the cake pan and place a cherry in the center of each pineapple slice. Pour the cake batter on top and smooth with an offset spatula. Bake until a toothpick

continued on page 86

continued from page 84

inserted into the center comes out clean, 40 to 45 minutes. Remove from the oven and let cool.

To make the cream: In the bowl of a stand mixer or in a bowl using a handheld mixer on high speed, beat the cream and granulated sugar until the cream is thick enough to form a dollop and hold its shape. Start beating on low speed until the cream becomes thick enough that it will not splatter on a higher speed.

Chop the remaining pineapple slice and mix half of it into the cream. Use the other half to garnish the top of each piece of cake.

Cut the cake into six pieces, cutting it so that each piece has a whole pineapple slice. Use a spatula to flip each piece onto a dessert plate so that the pineapple and cherry are visible. Top each piece of cake with a dollop of the pineapple cream, some of the chopped pineapple, and a maraschino cherry.

MERINGUE GLACÉ DAISIES

In the 1920s, meringue glacé was on the dessert menus in the fanciest restaurants in New York City like the ones that Daisy Buchanan and other ladies who lunched frequented. Meringue glacé is also a perfect nibble for high tea, like the tea that Nick arranged for Daisy and Jay Gatsby at his cottage.

The classic French dessert is light, cooling, and refreshing. It is also pretty to serve and can be presented in a variety of interesting ways. These meringue glacé daisies are made with meringue shaped like daisy petals arranged around a ball of ice cream covered in a bright yellow mirror glaze. Use the petals to scoop up the ice cream.

YIELD: 4 servings

MERINGUE

4 large egg whites

½ cup sugar

¼ teaspoon cream of tartar

MIRROR GLAZE

1¼ teaspoons powdered unflavored gelatin (half of 1 packet)

6 tablespoons water, divided

¾ cup sugar

¼ cup sweetened condensed milk

1 cup white chocolate chips

1 tablespoon yellow gel food coloring

4 cups vanilla ice cream

To make the meringue: Preheat the oven to 250°F. Line two baking sheets with parchment paper.

In the bowl of a stand mixer or in a bowl using a handheld mixer on high speed, beat the egg whites, sugar, and cream of tartar until the meringue becomes thickened and peaks form, 15 to 20 minutes.

Use a small ice cream scoop to form the meringue into 1-inch-round balls. Place 10 meringue balls, evenly spaced apart, on each of the prepared baking sheets. Use a large spoon to lightly flatten the top of each ball.

Bake until the meringue balls become firm enough so that they hold their shape when touched, 25 to 30 minutes. Remove the meringues from the oven and set them aside to cool.

To make the mirror glaze: In a small mixing bowl, combine the gelatin and 2 tablespoons of the water.

In a medium microwave-safe mixing bowl, combine the sugar, sweetened condensed milk, and remaining 4 tablespoons water. Microwave on high power for 1 minute. Remove and stir well to ensure the sugar is dissolved. Add the gelatin mixture and stir until the gelatin is completely dissolved.

In a separate medium microwave-safe mixing bowl, melt the white chocolate chips in the microwave on high power for 30 seconds. Remove and stir, then place back in the microwave for 5 seconds at a time until the chips are completely melted.

Add the melted white chocolate to the gelatin mixture and stir to combine. Set aside until the mixture reaches room temperature.

Add the food coloring, and mix well until there are no color streaks.

Use a large ice cream scoop to make 4 large round balls of ice cream. Place one ball of ice cream in the center of each dessert plate. Use a large spoon to pour one-fourth of the mirror glaze over each ball of ice cream.

Arrange 5 of the meringue daisy petals around each of the ice cream balls and serve immediately.

STRAWBERRY WHIPS

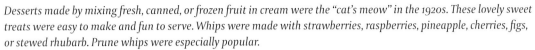

Desserts made by mixing fresh, canned, or frozen fruit in cream were the "cat's meow" in the 1920s. These lovely sweet treats were easy to make and fun to serve. Whips were made with strawberries, raspberries, pineapple, cherries, figs, or stewed rhubarb. Prune whips were especially popular.

Strawberry whips are best made with freshly picked strawberries at the height of summer, when berries are at their peak. Pick your own at a local berry farm.

This strawberry whip recipe appeared in The Charlotte Observer *(North Carolina) on August 22, 1925.*

YIELD: 4 servings

1 tablespoon plain gelatin

2 tablespoons cold water

2 egg whites*

1 cup powdered sugar

1 teaspoon vanilla extract

1 cup finely crushed strawberries

In a small bowl, soften the gelatin in the cold water and stir into egg whites.

In the bowl of a stand mixer or in a bowl using a handheld mixer on high speed, beat the egg whites until they become frothy, about 3 minutes. Gradually add the powdered sugar, followed by the vanilla, gelatin, and strawberries. Beat until stiff peaks form. Gently fold egg mixture into strawberry mixture.

Serve in clear glass dessert dishes or in cocktail glasses.

*You can use pasteurized egg whites.

NEW YORK–STYLE CHEESECAKE

A New York–style cheesecake is heavier on the cheese than other cheesecakes, like the dime store cheesecakes. Arnold Reuben created the now-classic New York cheesecake in the 1920s. Reuben owned Reuben's Restaurant and Delicatessen and the Turf Restaurant.

YIELD: 8 to 10 servings

CRUST

Cooking spray

12 graham crackers

5 tablespoons butter, melted

2½ tablespoons sugar

¼ teaspoon sea salt

FILLING

2 pounds cream cheese, softened

2 cups sugar

3 tablespoons all-purpose flour

4 teaspoons vanilla extract

½ teaspoon salt

8 small eggs

½ cup sour cream

SPECIALTY TOOLS

9-inch springform pan; large roasting pan

To make the crust: Wrap tinfoil all around the outside of the 9-inch round springform pan, being sure to cover the bottom well and pinching it together around the edges at the top to secure it. Spray the inside of the pan with cooking spray.

Chop the graham crackers into 1-inch pieces. In batches, crush them by pulsing them in a food processor.

In a large mixing bowl, combine the crushed crackers with the butter, sugar, and salt. Use a large spoon to mix well until all the crumbs are moistened. Press the cracker mixture into the bottom of the prepared pan, being careful to ensure that the mixture reaches every spot of the bottom of the pan.

To make the filling: Preheat the oven to 375°F.

In the bowl of a stand mixer or in a bowl using a handheld mixer on medium-high speed, beat the cream cheese, sugar, and flour until well combined and smooth, about 90 seconds. Add the vanilla and salt, and beat on low just until combined.

Add the eggs, one at a time, beating after each addition, until well combined. Add the sour cream and beat on low just until well combined, stopping occasionally to scrape down the sides of the mixing bowl. Pour the batter into the pan on top of the crust.

Place the pan in a large roasting pan and add water until it reaches about halfway up the sides of the cake pan. Bake until the cake is golden brown on top, 90 minutes to 2 hours. The cake will be jiggly because it needs to finish firming up in the refrigerator.

Place the cake in the refrigerator for 8 hours. Remove from the refrigerator. Remove the sides of the springform pan. Cut cheesecake into slices to serve.

DIME STORE CHEESECAKE

"'Plenty of gas,' said Tom boisterously. He looked at the gauge. 'And if it runs out I can stop at a drug-store. You can buy anything at a drug-store nowadays.'" —CHAPTER 7

In the late 1800s, chain corner drugstores—or "dime" stores, as they were often called—started popping up. By the time F. Scott Fitzgerald started writing The Great Gatsby, *many of them had luncheonettes, and thousands of them were in New York City. They served BLTs and plates of roast beef and mashed potatoes as big as your head. There was creamed chicken on toast, stewed tomatoes, and sandwiches of all kinds.*

This recipe is for a lemony, creamy cheesecake that became a staple of many lunch counters.

YIELD: 12 servings

CHEESECAKE

2 cups water

6 ounces powdered lemon-flavor gelatin

4 cups crushed graham crackers

1 cup butter

1½ cups heavy cream

1 cup sugar

Two 8-ounce packages cream cheese, softened

Juice of 5 large lemons

FRESH WHIPPED CREAM TOPPING

2 cups heavy cream

½ cup sugar

½ teaspoon fresh lemon juice

ASSEMBLY

2 cups cherry preserves, for topping

1 cup fresh mint leaves, for topping

To make the cheesecake: In a medium saucepan over high heat, bring the water to a boil. Add the powdered gelatin and stir until dissolved. Set aside to cool.

Pulse the graham crackers in a food processor. Melt the butter and mix in the crumbs until they are well covered. Pour the graham cracker mixture into a 9-by-13-inch cake pan. Using your hands, press all around on the bottom and sides of the cake pan to form a crust. Reserve some crumbs for a light topping.

Using a hand mixer in a large bowl, beat the cream and sugar until fluffy.

In a separate bowl, add the cream cheese, lemon juice, and gelatin mixture, and beat until combined. Gently fold in the whipped cream.

Pour the mixture over the crust in the cake pan. Sprinkle the reserved graham cracker crumbs on top. Cover with plastic wrap and chill the cheesecake in the refrigerator for at least 2 hours.

To make the fresh whipped cream topping: Using a stand mixer or in a bowl using a handheld mixer on high speed, beat the cream, sugar, and lemon juice until thickened, about 10 minutes on slow speed and increasing the speed as the cream thickens.

To assemble: Serve the cake with the whipped cream topping, cherry preserves, and fresh mint leaf on each piece.

LAZY DAISY CAKE

In March 1925, the Snowdrift shortening company published its brand-new recipe in all of the newspapers. The recipe was for a light, fluffy yellow cake with a sweet, lightly crunchy coating of coconut, butter, and brown sugar melted into the top.

Suddenly, lazy daisy cake was everywhere. The cake was trendy for many years and was a favorite in most households throughout the roaring twenties and well into the 1930s.

This cake gets sprigs of fresh garden-grown lavender as a garnish. The bright purple-blue color offsets the very plain color of the cake. Add sliced peaches or other stone fruits, or pineapple or apple slices, for a Lazy Daisy Upside-Down Cake.

YIELD: 12 servings

CAKE

1 teaspoon butter, plus more for the pan

2 eggs

1 cup granulated sugar

¼ teaspoon salt

1 teaspoon vanilla extract

1 cup all-purpose flour

1 teaspoon baking powder

½ cup milk

TOPPING

1 cup sweetened shredded coconut

2 tablespoons milk

2 tablespoons butter, melted

⅓ cup brown sugar

To make the cake: Preheat the oven to 350°F. Generously grease and flour a 9-inch round or square cake pan with butter.

In a large mixing bowl, use a fork to lightly beat the eggs until thick and lemon-color. Gradually add the granulated sugar and beat with a handheld mixer for 5 minutes. Beat in the salt and vanilla. Add the flour and baking powder and beat to combine.

In a medium saucepan over high heat, scald the milk and 1 teaspoon butter until melted, and add the mixture to the batter. Pour the batter into the prepared pan and bake until a toothpick inserted into the center comes out clean, about 30 minutes.

To make the topping: While the cake is baking, add the topping ingredients to a large mixing bowl and stir to combine.

Remove the cake from the oven and, while it is still hot, spread the topping over the cake. Return the cake to the oven and bake until the topping turns lightly brown, 2 to 3 minutes. Watch carefully so the topping does not become too brown. Remove from the oven and let cool before serving.

LADY BALTIMORE CAKE

▽

"A breeze blew through the room, blew curtains in at one end and out the other like pale flags, twisting them up toward the frosted wedding-cake of the ceiling, and then rippled over the wine-colored rug, making a shadow on it as wind does on the sea." —CHAPTER I

Voluptuous with layers of cake piled high, fluffy frosting, and candied fruits and nuts, Lady Baltimore cake was the wedding cake of choice for many couples years ago.

There are as many stories handed down about the origins of Lady Baltimore cake as there are dried fruits and nuts in the filling of this decadent dessert. A widely believed theory is the story of Owen Wister in 1906. Wister was in Charleston, South Carolina, working on his romance novel, Lady Baltimore. *Wister wrote about the cake, saying it reminded him of a wedding cake. Here is what Wister wrote about the Lady Baltimore Cake: "'I should like a slice, if you please, of Lady Baltimore,' I said with extreme formality. I thought she was going to burst; but after an interesting second she replied, 'Certainly,' in her fit regular-exchange tone; only, I thought it trembled a little. I returned to the table and she brought me the cake, and I had my first felicitous meeting with Lady Baltimore. Oh, my goodness! Did you ever taste it? It's all soft, and it's in layers, and it has nuts—but I can't write any more about it; my mouth waters too much!"*

YIELD: 12 servings

CAKE

½ cup butter, plus more for the pan

1½ cups granulated sugar

1 cup milk

3 cups flour, plus more for the pan

2 teaspoons baking powder

4 egg whites, stiffly beaten

1 teaspoon vanilla extract

FROSTING AND FILLING

3 egg whites

¼ teaspoon pink Himalayan sea salt

1½ cups granulated sugar

⅔ cup water

2 teaspoons light corn syrup

1 teaspoon vanilla extract

½ cup pecans, chopped

½ cup figs, chopped

½ cup raisins

½ cup candied cherries

½ cup candied pineapple

To make the cake: Preheat the oven to 350°F. Butter and flour three 8-inch round cake pans.

In the bowl of a stand mixer or in a large mixing bowl using a handheld mixer on high speed, cream the butter and sugar until light and fluffy. Gradually add the milk, beating to combine. Add the flour and baking powder. Fold in the stiffly beaten egg whites and the vanilla.

Divide the cake batter among the prepared cake pans and smooth the batter with an offset spatula. Bake until a toothpick inserted into the centers come out clean, 25 minutes. Remove from the oven and let cool. Turn out the cakes onto a wire rack to cool completely.

To make the frosting and filling: In the bowl of a stand mixer or in a large mixing bowl using a handheld mixer on high speed, beat the egg whites until stiff peaks form. Add the salt and beat to combine. Set aside.

continued on page 96

continued from page 95

In a small saucepan over medium heat, combine the sugar, water, and corn syrup, stirring occasionally. Once the mixture comes to a boil, continue stirring, more frequently, until the sugar is dissolved.

Boil the syrup until it registers 248°F on a candy thermometer. Remove the syrup from the heat, and immediately pour a very thin stream over the stiffly beaten egg whites, beating constantly. Add the vanilla and continue beating until the frosting is fluffy and holds its shape.

Remove one-third of the frosting to a bowl. Add the chopped nuts and fruit to it, reserving some for garnish, and stir to combine. Apply this between each cake layer and on the top. Frost the top and the sides of the cake with the remaining frosting. Sprinkle the reserved nuts and fruit on top to garnish.

PEARL NECKLACE TAPIOCA CUPS

"I shook hands with him; it seemed silly not to, for I felt suddenly as though I were talking to a child. Then he went into the jewelry store to buy a pearl necklace—or perhaps only a pair of cuff buttons—rid of my provincial squeamishness forever." —CHAPTER 9

The pearl necklaces of the flappers at Jay Gatsby's parties shook as they shimmied to dances like the Charleston, the Fox Trot, and more.

In the summer of 1925, recipes for refreshing cups of pudding made with tapioca pearls ran in newspapers across the United States. Served in individual dishes, the fashionable dessert became known as tapioca cups.

This version gets a decadent drizzle of fresh raspberry coulis for an extra zip of flavor and a shot of vibrant color.

YIELD: 4 to 6 servings

TAPIOCA

One 8-ounce box instant tapioca

1 large egg

2 cups whole milk

1 teaspoon vanilla extract

6 tablespoons sugar

RASPBERRY COULIS

2 cups fresh raspberries

3 tablespoons orange juice

1 tablespoon Grand Marnier

1 cup fresh mint leaves

To make the tapioca: Working with the ingredients listed here, cook the tapioca according to the directions on the box.

To make the raspberry coulis: In a medium saucepan over high heat, combine the raspberries, orange juice, and Grand Marnier. Bring to a boil, reduce the heat to medium, and cook until a thickened syrup forms, 15 to 20 minutes. Stir occasionally. Remove from the heat and set aside to cool. Pour the coulis through a fine-mesh strainer into a medium bowl and discard the raspberry seeds.

Serve the tapioca in clear glass dessert cups or cocktail glasses, with a drizzle of coulis and a few fresh fresh mint leaves on each dessert.

BRANDIED FRUIT COCKTAIL

During Prohibition, resourceful restaurateurs served fruit salads, shrimp, and crab in cocktail glasses that would otherwise collect dust. The presentations were colorful, elegant, and inviting. A new trend in entertaining was set that continues to this day. Some believe the terms "fruit cocktail" and "seafood cocktail" are derived from the use of the cocktail glasses to serve these popular treats.

A big, beautiful sprig of fresh peppermint and some fresh whipped cream are nice accents for a fruit cocktail loaded with plump candied cherries, diced pears and peaches, and pineapple chunks. This recipe is a perfect way to celebrate fruits at the peak of the season at a summer party.

YIELD: 8 to 10 servings

2 cups applejack brandy

1 cup pitted cherries

1 cup diced peaches

1 cup peeled and chopped oranges

1 cup peeled and chopped grapefruit

1 cup green grapes

2 cups sugar

6 cups vanilla ice cream

2 cups fresh mint leaves

In a large mixing bowl, place the brandy, fruit, and sugar; cover with plastic wrap and chill in the refrigerator for 8 to 12 hours.

Place a large scoop of ice cream in a clear glass dessert dish and spoon the fruit and its juices on top. Garnish with the fresh mint.

NEAPOLITAN ICE CREAM

Ice creams weren't new in the 1920s, but the increased availability of iceboxes (refrigerators) in homes made frozen desserts everyday household treats for the first time ever. One of the most popular ice cream varieties was Neapolitan, which is made by layering vanilla, chocolate, and strawberry ice creams.

This Neapolitan ice cream is made with fresh vanilla beans, Belgian chocolate, and freshly picked strawberries. Top each serving of this nostalgic dessert with a fresh sprig of chocolate mint.

YIELD: 10 servings

2 vanilla beans

3¼ cups heavy cream, divided

1 cup good-quality chocolate chips, such as Valrhona

3 tablespoons sugar

14 ounces sweetened condensed milk

2 cups chopped strawberries

Fresh chocolate mint sprigs, for garnish

Line a 9-by-4-inch loaf pan with parchment paper.

Split the vanilla beans, and use a table knife to scrape the vanilla seeds from the inside of each pod. In a small saucepan over medium-high heat, combine the vanilla bean seeds and pods with ¼ cup of the cream. Stir to blend and infuse the cream, about 10 minutes. Remove from the heat, remove the vanilla bean pods and set aside to cool.

Place the chocolate chips in a medium microwave-safe bowl and microwave on high power until melted, about 90 seconds.

In the bowl of a stand mixer or in a bowl using a handheld mixer on medium-high speed, beat the remaining 3 cups cream with the sugar until thickened, 15 to 20 minutes. Start on low speed until the cream thickens enough so that it won't splatter when it is on a higher speed.

Divide the whipped cream evenly among three medium mixing bowls. Place one-third of the sweetened condensed milk into each of the bowls and stir lightly just until folded in. Fold in the cooled vanilla cream to the cream in one bowl, the strawberries to another, and the melted chocolate to the third.

Spread the strawberry cream on the bottom of the prepared loaf pan and place in the freezer until solid, 4 to 6 hours. Cover the vanilla and chocolate creams with plastic wrap and chill in the refrigerator.

When the strawberry cream is frozen, spread the vanilla cream evenly on top. Place in the freezer until solid, 4 to 6 hours.

When the vanilla cream is frozen, spread the chocolate cream evenly on top. Place in the freezer until solid, 4 to 6 hours.

Run a large knife under hot water and use it to slice the dessert widthwise into 1-inch-thick slices. Lay each slice flat so that the colors are visible. Garnish each with a sprig of chocolate mint.

FESTIVE SIPS FOR TIPPLERS AND TEETOTALERS

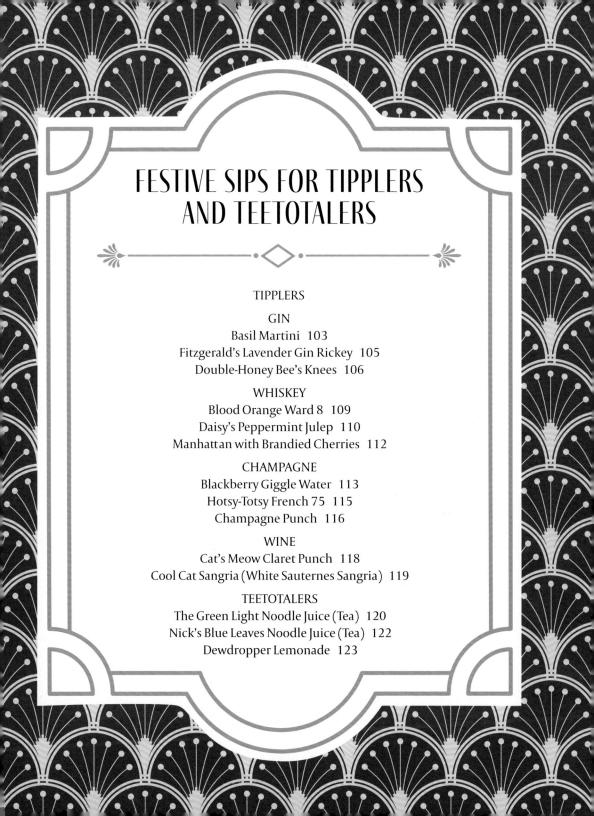

TIPPLERS

GIN
Basil Martini 103
Fitzgerald's Lavender Gin Rickey 105
Double-Honey Bee's Knees 106

WHISKEY
Blood Orange Ward 8 109
Daisy's Peppermint Julep 110
Manhattan with Brandied Cherries 112

CHAMPAGNE
Blackberry Giggle Water 113
Hotsy-Totsy French 75 115
Champagne Punch 116

WINE
Cat's Meow Claret Punch 118
Cool Cat Sangria (White Sauternes Sangria) 119

TEETOTALERS
The Green Light Noodle Juice (Tea) 120
Nick's Blue Leaves Noodle Juice (Tea) 122
Dewdropper Lemonade 123

HIGHBALLS

As Gatsby, Nick, and Mr. Wolfsheim walked into a lunch place in New York City (chapter 4), the head waiter asked: "Highballs?"

"This is a nice restaurant here," said Mr. Wolfsheim, looking at the Presbyterian nymphs on the ceiling. "But I like across the street better!"

"Yes, highballs," agreed Gatsby, and then to Mr. Wolfsheim: "It's too hot over there."

"Hot and small—yes," said Mr. Wolfsheim, "but full of memories."

"What place is that?" I asked.

"The old Metropole."

Later, in another gathering, highballs were also served: "Mr. Sloane didn't enter into the conversation, but lounged back haughtily in his chair; the woman said nothing either—until unexpectedly, after two highballs, she became cordial."

Highballs are a mix of booze and soda. They can be whiskey and ginger ale, or gin and tonic, or another concoction.

GIN

"In the main hall a bar with a real brass rail was set up, and stocked with gins and liquors and ..." —CHAPTER 3

BASIL MARTINI

Fitzgerald wrote much of his 1922 short story "Mr. Icky" while staying at the Knickerbocker Hotel in New York City. There are many theories of where the "king of cocktails"—the martini—was invented. The closest story related to Fitzgerald is that Knickerbocker bartender Martini di Arma di Taggia created a new drink in 1906 to knock the socks off of John D. Rockefeller. Rockefeller was said to have loved the drink right away and dubbed it "the Martini." Word spread quickly around the world, and the drink is still one of the most popular cocktails in history.

This recipe adds fresh garden notes by including chopped fresh basil in the shaker with the ice and other ingredients. It is important to chop the basil to release its flavorful oils. Add a sprig of basil with the tiniest leaves for garnish.

YIELD: 1 serving

2 ounces dry gin

6 fresh basil leaves, chiffonade, plus one sprig basil, for garnish

1 ounce dry vermouth

2 dashes angostura or orange bitters

1 cup ice

1 spicy pimento-stuffed olive, for garnish

Combine the gin, chiffonade basil, vermouth, bitters, and ice in a cocktail shaker and shake for 30 revolutions. Strain the cocktail into a martini glass. Garnish with a spicy pimento-stuffed olive and the sprig of basil on a cocktail pick.

FITZGERALD'S LAVENDER GIN RICKEY

"With a reluctant backward glance the well-disciplined child held to her nurse's hand and was pulled out the door, just as Tom came back, preceding four gin rickeys that clicked full of ice. Gatsby took up his drink. 'They certainly look cool,' he said, with visible tension. We drank in long greedy swallows. 'I read somewhere that the sun's getting hotter every year,' said Tom genially. 'It seems that pretty soon the earth's going to fall into the sun—or wait a minute—it's just the opposite— the sun's getting colder every year.'" —CHAPTER 7

It's not surprising that Fitzgerald celebrated the gin rickey in his stories, as it was his favorite cocktail. This recipe celebrates Gatsby's impressive gardens with a hint of lavender that adds flavor and color to the classic gin rickey. Grow lavender in a garden or window box to make this simple syrup with sugar and water. Save some sprigs to plop between the ice cubes as garnish. Sprinkle some loose lavender on top.

YIELD: 1 serving

LAVENDER SIMPLE SYRUP

½ cup fresh or dried lavender buds

½ cup water

½ cup granulated sugar

COCKTAIL

½ cup ice

2 ounces dry gin

½ cup club soda

1 teaspoon fresh lime juice

2 ounces lavender simple syrup

1 lime wheel or slice

To make the lavender simple syrup: In a medium saucepan over high heat, stir together the lavender, water, and sugar until the sugar is dissolved. Bring to a boil, and reduce the heat to low. Simmer for 15 minutes. Remove the saucepan from the heat, and use a fine-mesh strainer to strain the lavender from the liquid. Place the liquid in a heat-proof container and set it on the countertop to cool. When it is cool enough to transfer to the refrigerator, place the syrup in an airtight container until it is chilled.

To make the cocktail: Fill a Tom Collins glass with ice and add the gin, club soda, lime juice, and lavender simple syrup. Use a barspoon to stir rapidly for about 30 revolutions. Garnish with the lime wheel.

DOUBLE-HONEY BEE'S KNEES

During Prohibition, 1920 to 1933, bathtub gin—or homemade booze—was as popular as bucket hats and Bakelite jewelry. Adding honey to cocktails masked the bitter taste of bootlegged alcohol and became as trendy as the bob hairdo. Flappers developed new expressions by relating impressive things to animals, like "the cat's pajamas" or "hot dog." They called a sweet, new cocktail made with gin, honey, and lemon "the bee's knees."

This bee's knees recipe makes the classic Prohibition cocktail even sweeter, because it is made with honey syrup that has twice as much honey as traditional recipes. Lemon juice makes this bright and citrusy. Fresh mint adds a crisp flavor.

YIELD: 1 serving

HONEY SYRUP

1 cup honey

½ cup water

1 cup chopped fresh mint

COCKTAIL

Ice

2 ounces gin

1½ ounces honey syrup

½ ounce fresh lemon juice

1 fresh mint leaf

1 long, thin strip lemon peel

To make the honey syrup: In a small saucepan, bring the honey and water to a boil. Reduce the heat to a simmer and add the mint. Simmer for 12 to 15 minutes. Set the syrup aside on the countertop to cool to room temperature, about 20 minutes. Strain the syrup through a fine-mesh strainer into a medium bowl; discard the mint. Store the syrup in an airtight container in the refrigerator for up to 1 month.

To make the cocktail: In a cocktail shaker filled with ice, add the gin, honey syrup, and lemon juice, and shake for approximately 30 revolutions. Strain into a coupe glass and serve with the mint leaf and lemon peel.

WHISKEY

"The bottle of whiskey—a second one—was now in constant demand by all present, excepting Catherine, who 'felt just as good on nothing at all.'...Tom brought out a bottle of whiskey from a locked bureau door. I have been drunk just twice in my life, and the second time was that afternoon; so everything that happened has a dim, hazy cast over it, although until after eight o'clock the apartment was full of cheerful sun." —CHAPTER 2

"Daisy called down 'Shall we take anything to drink?' 'I'll get some whiskey,' answered Tom. He went inside. Later, in the hotel in the city, the whiskey was unrolled from a towel and set on a table.

Tom got up and began wrapping the unopened bottle of whiskey in the towel. 'Want any of this stuff? Jordan?… Nick?' 'Nick?' 'What?' 'Want any?' 'No…I just remembered that to-day's my birthday.'"

BLOOD ORANGE WARD 8

The Ward 8 cocktail was invented in 1898 at the now-shuttered Locke-Ober Café in the eighth ward in Boston.

YIELD: 1 serving

2 ounces whiskey

½ ounce fresh lemon juice

½ ounce fresh orange juice

1 teaspoon grenadine

1 teaspoon blood orange liqueur or syrup

¼ cup ice

1 or 2 brandied cherries

Combine the whiskey, lemon juice, orange juice, grenadine, blood orange liqueur, and ice in a cocktail shaker and shake for 30 revolutions. Strain the cocktail into a coupe glass. Garnish with cherries on a cocktail pick.

How to Make Brandied Cherries

1 cup fresh cherries, pitted and trimmed

1 cup brandy

½ cup sugar

In a large bowl, combine the cherries, brandy, and sugar. Cover and refrigerate for 8 to 12 hours. Strain the cherries from the liquid to use as garnish. Discard the liquid.

DAISY'S PEPPERMINT JULEP

On a steamy day in New York City that was hot enough to prompt Daisy to quip about hiring five bathrooms to take cold baths, she suggested finding "a place to have a mint julep." The Louisville, Kentucky, native was no doubt familiar with the refreshing qualities of an ice-filled glass of the very Southern cocktail.

"'Call up and order some ice for the mint julep,' Daisy ordered Tom.

"Daisy rose, smiling faintly, and went to the table. 'Open the whiskey, Tom,' she ordered, 'and I'll make you a mint julep. Then you won't seem so stupid to yourself…Look at the mint!'"

U.S. senator Henry Clay was said to have introduced the cocktail in Washington, D.C., in 1850, and President Theodore Roosevelt loved the drink. By 1938, the mint julep was the official cocktail of the Kentucky Derby.

The fresh peppermint in this recipe heightens the mintiness and adds a special spark of fresh flavor to the classic mint julep.

YIELD: 1 serving

2½ ounces whiskey

2 ounces soda water

1 teaspoon sugar

3 dashes angostura or orange bitters

1 cup ice

½ cup fresh peppermint or other mint leaves, plus more for garnish

Combine the whiskey, soda water, sugar, bitters, ice, and peppermint in a cocktail shaker and shake for 30 revolutions. Pour cocktail into a julep cup or Tom Collins glass. Garnish with additional mint.

MANHATTAN WITH BRANDIED CHERRIES

"When I came back they had disappeared so I sat down discreetly in the living room and read a chapter of *Simon Called Peter*—either it was terrible stuff or the whiskey distorted things because it didn't make any sense to me. Just as Tom and Myrtle—after the first drink Mrs. Wilson and I called each other by our first names—reappeared, company commenced to arrive at the apartment door." —CHAPTER 2

While there is no mention of them in The Great Gatsby, *Manhattan cocktails must have flowed at Jay Gatsby's poolside parties. The Manhattan has been one of the most distinguished mixed drinks in the world for hundreds of years—so historic is its origins that its inventor remains a mystery. The basic recipe has remained unchanged throughout the years and is no doubt how Gatsby's guests would have enjoyed it. The Manhattan is made with bourbon whiskey, sweet vermouth, and a few splashes of bitters for herbal notes of flavor.*

This recipe features brandied cherries. While they require a bit of planning and preparation, they truly make the most fitting garnish for this classic cocktail. In a pinch, maraschino cherries will work almost as well. Pick cherries at the height of summer when they are in season, and let them soak until the holidays. They are wonderful gifts, with a recipe book and some ingredients.

YIELD: 1 serving

2 ounces whiskey

1 ounce sweet vermouth

5 dashes angostura or orange bitters

1 cup ice

1 brandied cherry (page 109)

Combine the whiskey, vermouth, bitters, and ice in a cocktail shaker and shake for 30 revolutions. Strain the cocktail into a coupe glass or a martini glass.

CHAMPAGNE

"In his blue gardens men and girls came and went like moths among the whisperings and the Champagne and the stars." —CHAPTER 3

BLACKBERRY GIGGLE WATER

While there was plenty of Champagne flowing at his parties, Gatsby abstained: "It was indirectly due to Cody that Gatsby drank so little. Sometimes in the course of gay parties women used to rub Champagne into his hair; for himself he formed the habit of letting liquor alone."

"...with cordials so long forgotten that most of his female guests were too young to know one from another." —CHAPTER 3

1920s flappers called Champagne cocktails "giggle water." Here is a refreshing recipe for a giggle water made with fresh blackberries and mint.

YIELD: 4 servings

BLACKBERRY SIMPLE SYRUP

½ cup fresh blackberries, plus 8 extra for garnish

½ cup granulated sugar

½ cup water

GIGGLE WATER

4 cups ice

1 (750-ml) bottle Champagne or sparkling wine

12 fresh mint leaves

To make the blackberry simple syrup: In a medium saucepan over high heat, combine blackberries, the sugar, and water, and bring to a boil. Reduce the heat to medium-high and simmer the ingredients until they thicken into a syrup consistency, 10 to 15 minutes.

Remove the syrup from the heat and set on the countertop to cool. Strain the syrup through a fine-mesh strainer into a small bowl. Discard the blackberry seeds. Set the syrup in the refrigerator to cool.

To make the giggle water: Fill 4 wineglasses or Champagne flutes halfway with ice. Pour one-fourth of the syrup into each glass, followed by one-fourth of the Champagne.

Garnish with a plump blackberry and a few fresh mint leaves on a cocktail pick.

HOTSY-TOTSY FRENCH 75

"By midnight the hilarity had increased. A celebrated tenor had sung in Italian and a notorious contralto had sung in jazz and between the numbers people were doing 'stunts' all over the garden, while happy vacuous bursts of laughter rose toward the summer sky ... I was still with Jordan Baker. We were sitting at a table with a man of about my age and a rowdy little girl who gave way upon the slightest provocation to uncontrollable laughter. I was enjoying myself now. I had taken of Champagne and the scene had changed before my eyes into something significant, elemental and profound." —CHAPTER 3

The French 75 is a Champagne cocktail. It was one of the most desirable cocktails of Prohibition, when anything that was especially pleasing was dubbed "hotsy-totsy." The name of the drink was inspired by France's 1897 model 75 canon. Barman Harry MacElhone invented the French 75—or "Soixante Quinze" in French—at Harry's New York Bar in Paris during World War I. At that time, the now-venerated establishment was called the New York Bar. In the 1920s, from Paris to New York and everywhere in between, the French 75 cocktail was one of the most popular tipples.

This variation of the cocktail is a mix of Champagne, gin, fresh lemon juice, and maple syrup. Garnish this French 75 with a slender, curly lemon peel and a sprig of fresh lemon thyme.

YIELD: 1 serving

1 cup ice

2 ounces Champagne
or sparkling wine

2 ounces dry gin

1 ounce maple syrup

½ teaspoon fresh lemon juice

1 thin slice lemon peel, for garnish

1 sprig fresh thyme, for garnish

Place the ice in a wine glass or broad Champagne flute. Add the Champagne, gin, syrup, and lemon juice. Garnish with the lemon peel and fresh thyme sprig.

CHAMPAGNE PUNCH

▼

"A pair of stage twins, who turned out to be the girls in yellow, did a baby act in costume, and Champagne was served in glasses bigger than finger-bowls. The moon had risen higher, and floating in the Sound was a triangle of silver scales, trembling a little to the stiff, tinny drip of the banjoes on the lawn." —CHAPTER 3

In July 1925, Mrs. Walter Shiers won first place in The Springfield News-Sun (Ohio) drink recipe contest. Her recipe for "Oriental Punch" featured brewed tea in a punch. With whole cloves as an accent, and lots of orange juice and grape juice, her punch is a lemony refreshment that brings a touch of the jazz age to any party.

This recipe, which includes Champagne (hers did not), is an adaptation of Mrs. Shiers' summertime treat.

YIELD: 12 to 14 servings

4 cups lemon-lime tea

4 cups boiling water

12 whole cloves

4 lemons

1 (750-ml) bottle Champagne or sparkling wine

½ cup sugar

1 cup orange juice

3 cups ice

6 cups orange sherbet, divided

In a kettle, steep the tea and the whole cloves in the water for about 10 minutes.

Slice the lemons and place them in a large bowl. Pour the tea over the lemons. Let sit until cool, 20 to 30 minutes.

Meanwhile, in a large punch bowl, combine the Champagne, sugar, orange juice, ice, and 3 cups of the sherbet. Reserve the remaining 3 cups sherbet to refresh the punch bowl later.

Strain the tea through a fine-mesh strainer into the punch bowl, and stir to combine.

WINE

"In his blue gardens men and girls came and went like moths among the whisperings and the Champagne and the stars." —CHAPTER 3

CAT'S MEOW CLARET PUNCH

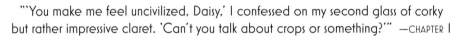

"'You make me feel uncivilized, Daisy,' I confessed on my second glass of corky but rather impressive claret. 'Can't you talk about crops or something?'" —CHAPTER 1

Claret is a red wine from the Bordeaux region in France. Two popular clarets are cabernet sauvignon and merlot. While they are wonderful to sip on their own, clarets are also perfect in sangrias or punches.

In the 1920s, this claret punch would have been declared the "cat's meow" for its full-bodied flavor and complex range of fruitiness. Serve this in a large, clear glass punch bowl with a sizable chunk of ice with cabernet or merlot grapes floating in it for a dramatic presentation. Add large spoonfuls of raspberry sherbet to the punch bowl to melt into the punch and create a delicious foam.

YIELD: 12 to 14 servings

1 (750-ml) bottle cabernet sauvignon or merlot wine

4 cups lemon-lime soda

2 cups ice

2 cups red and green grapes

6 cups raspberry sherbet

In a large punch bowl, combine all the ingredients and stir.

COOL CAT SANGRIA
(WHITE SAUTERNES SANGRIA)

"Every Friday five crates of oranges and lemons arrived from a fruitier in New York—every Monday these same oranges and lemons left his back door in a pyramid of pulpless halves. There was a machine in the kitchen which could extract the juice of two hundred oranges in half an hour if a little button was pressed two hundred times by a butler's thumb." —CHAPTER 3

Rich with fresh oranges and lemons, this sangria—so delicious it earns the 1920s' "cool cat" reference—is made with sauternes. Sauternes are sweet white wines that are referenced in The Great Gatsby. *Jordan Baker recalled one of the only times when Daisy overindulged, which was on the night before her wedding:*

"I came into her room half an hour before the bridal dinner, and found her lying on her bed as lovely as the June night in her flowered dress—and as drunk as a monkey. She had a bottle of sauterne in one hand and a letter in the other. 'Gratulate me,' she muttered. 'Never had a drink before, but oh how I do enjoy it.'" —CHAPTER 4

YIELD: 12 to 14 servings

1 12.5-ounce bottle white sauternes wine

4 cups lemon-lime soda

2 cups ice

2 cups grapefruit juice

2 cups orange juice

4 lemon slices

4 lime slices, plus more for garnish

3 grapefruit slices

In a large pitcher or a punch bowl, combine all the ingredients and stir. Garnish each glass with a lime slice.

TEETOTALERS

"In his blue gardens men and girls came and went like moths among the whisperings and the Champagne and the stars." —CHAPTER 3

THE GREEN LIGHT NOODLE JUICE (TEA)

▽

"And as I sat there brooding on the old, unknown world, I thought of Gatsby's wonder when he first picked out the green light at the end of Daisy's dock. He had come a long way to this blue lawn and his dream must have seemed so close that he could hardly fail to grasp it. He did not know that it was already behind him, somewhere back in that vast obscurity beyond the city, where the dark fields of the republic rolled on under the night. Gatsby believed in the green light, the orgastic future that year by year recedes before us. It eluded us then, but that's no matter—tomorrow we will run faster, stretch out our arms farther. ... And one fine morning—so we beat on, boats against the current, borne back ceaselessly into the past." —CHAPTER 9

The green light is one of the prevailing symbols of The Great Gatsby. From across the water, shining constantly like a beacon of unfailing hope from Daisy's dock, Jay Gatsby can see the green light.

During the 1920s, the term "noodle juice" became a new moniker for tea. This recipe includes drops of green food coloring to make a minty tea that is as pronounced in color as the green light from Daisy's dock. The flavor is distinct as well.

Make this tea cold for a hot summer afternoon or warm for an evening curled up with a classic book.

YIELD: 1 serving

1 tablespoon mint tea

1 cup hot water

½ teaspoon lime juice

¼ teaspoon honey

Green food coloring

1 lime slice

1 sprig fresh mint

In a teacup, steep the tea in the hot water. Add the lime juice, honey and a drop of the green food coloring, and stir. Garnish with a slice of lime and fresh mint.

Opposite Page: The Green Light Noodle Juice (left); Nick's Blue Leaves Noodle Juice recipe, page 122 (right)

NICK'S BLUE LEAVES NOODLE JUICE (TEA)

"It was dawn now on Long Island and we went about opening the rest of the windows down-stairs, filling the house with gray-turning, gold-turning light. The shadow of a tree fell abruptly across the dew and ghostly birds began to sing among the blue leaves. There was a slow, pleasant movement in the air, scarcely a wind, promising a cool, lovely day." —CHAPTER 8

Butterfly pea flower in this noodle juice—or tea—naturally provides the color of the blue leaves at Gatsby's impressive estate. This tea is delicious sipped in the garden, either iced or warm. Garnish it with the tiniest blooms of blue cornflowers or lavender, or with the littlest star-shape buds of blue borage. The colorful flowers provide contrasting deep, vibrant hues of purplish blue.

YIELD: 1 serving

1 tablespoon butterfly
pea flower tea

1 teaspoon lavender buds

1 cup hot water

¼ teaspoon sugar

In a teacup, steep the tea and lavender in the hot water. Add the sugar and stir.

DEWDROPPER LEMONADE

"'Sit right down. Have a cigarette or a cigar.' He walked around the room quickly, ringing bells. 'I'll have something to drink for you in just a minute.' He was profoundly affected by the fact that Tom was there. But he would be uneasy anyhow until he had given them something, realizing in a vague way that that was all they came for. Mr. Sloane wanted nothing. A lemonade? No, thanks. A little champagne? Nothing at all, thanks." —CHAPTER 6

When it's a tea for an especially lazy summer day, it's called dewdropper tea. During the jazz age—a reference coined by F. Scott Fitzgerald—someone lazily wasting away the day would have been labeled a dewdropper.

This dewdropper lemonade is a delicious thirst-quencher on its own or spiked with a little Champagne. In chapter 6, Gatsby offers Tom and his riding group a choice: "Mr. Sloane wanted nothing. A lemonade? No, thanks. A little champagne? Nothing at all, thanks…"

Garnish this lemony drink with a thin slice of lemon and some fresh lemon thyme on the side of the glass. This should be sipped slowly in the garden and enjoyed on the the most restful days of summer.

YIELD: 1 serving

1 cup ginger ale

5 lemon slices, plus more for garnish

½ cup ice cubes

1 sprig fresh or dried lemon thyme, for garnish

In a Tom Collins glass, combine the ginger ale, lemon slices, and ice, and stir with a cocktail stirrer. Garnish with lemon thyme.

ENTERTAINING GUIDE

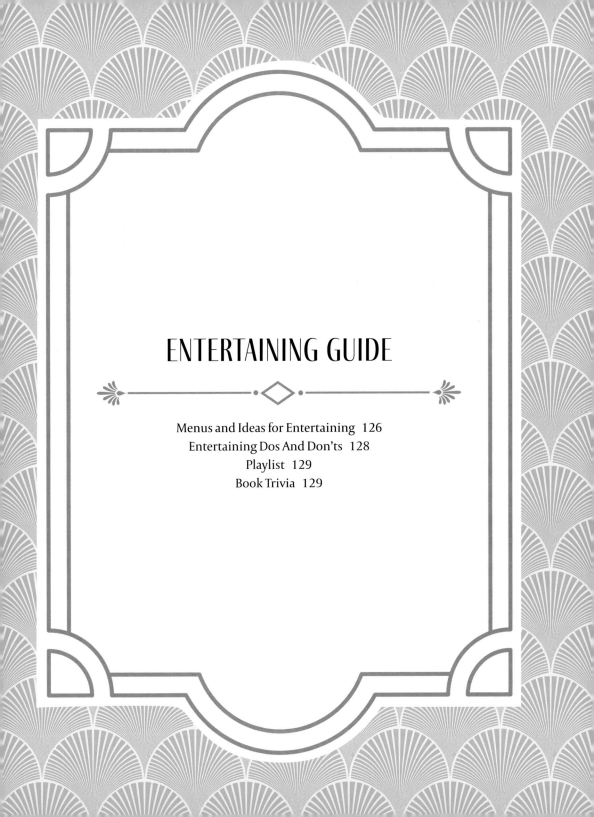

MENUS AND IDEAS FOR ENTERTAINING

SUMMER SOLSTICE GARDEN PARTY

Gatsby's Pastry Pigs with Grape Jelly and Mint *(page 14)*

Swedish Meatballs with Lingonberry Sauce *(page 21)*

Waldorf Salad Bites *(page 22)*

Cold Crab Dip *(page 24)*

Smoked Whitefish Dip *(page 33)*

Bacon and Horseradish Cheeseball *(page 32)*

Pineapple-Lime Gelatin Salad *(page 46)*

Cranberry Fluff Salad *(page 52)*

Gatsby's Spiced Baked Ham with Champagne Sauce *(page 57)*

New York–Style Cheesecake *(page 90)*

Brandied Fruit Cocktail *(page 98)*

MOTHER'S DAY TEA PARTY

Nick's High-Tea Finger Sandwiches: Strawberry-Mint, Cilantro-Radish, Tarragon-Carrot, Garlicky Cucumber, Honey-Roasted Garden Beet *(page 75)*

Daisy's Lemon Cakes *(page 83)*

FATHER'S DAY PORCH LUNCH

Deviled Eggs *(page 28)*

Quick Pickled Carrots *(page 29)*

Consommé Madrilene *(page 41)*

Julia Arthur Salad *(page 49)*

Tom and Daisy's Cold Fried Chicken *(page 63)*

Strawberry Whips *(page 89)*

THANKSGIVING (OR "FRIENDSGIVING") DINNER PARTY

Shrimp Cocktail *(page 31)*

Manhattan Clam Chowder *(page 42)*

Frozen Tomato Salad *(page 43)*

42nd Street Cellar "Succulent" Hash *(page 37)*

Gatsby's Lemon-Roasted Turkey *(page 60)*

Lady Baltimore Cake *(page 95)*

VALENTINE'S DAY DINNER

Baked West Egg Oysters Rockefeller *(page 17)*

Alligator Pear Salad *(page 50)*

Boiled Beet Greens and Crispy Bacon *(page 38)*

42nd Street Cellar "Succulent" Hash *(page 37)*

Scott and Zelda's Pale Ale–Braised Pork Chops with Stewed Green Apples *(page 67)*

Meringue Glacé Daisies *(page 87)*

PARTY GAMES

PARCHEESI Parcheesi is a board game with four players. Each player has four game pieces. The objective is to get all four game pieces into the center of the game board. Dice are rolled to determine which game pieces can be moved.

POKER Poker is a card game with the objective to get the best five-card hand.

GIN RUMMY Gin Rummy is a card game with two players. The objective is to be the first player to reach a score of usually 100 points.

CRAPS Craps is a game of luck that requires no skill. Players roll two dice and keep track of points throughout each game. Bets can be placed on the outcome of each dice roll.

ROULETTE The objective of roulette is to spin a ball in a wheel on a table and place bets on where the ball will land.

DANCES

CHARLESTON The Charleston is a step forward, step back dance with feet and knees twisting and arms swinging up and down and side to side.

BLACK BOTTOM The Black Bottom includes two moves. In the first move, dancers hold their hands together and touch each knee, lifting each leg, alternately. In the second move, dancers reach both hands in the air to the side while side-stepping with their feet.

SHIMMY This partner dance was considered provocative at the time because of how the two-stepping moves made the dancers shake.

FOXTROT In this dance, partners take long, graceful strides together throughout the dance floor. The dance includes slow stepping mixed with quick stepping.

TEXAS TOMMY Some consider the Texas Tommy to be the first swing dance, because it is an eight-step partner dance that includes a breakaway step. Dancers kick and hop three times on each foot, and then slide into a breakaway that inspires acrobatics and other showy moves.

ENTERTAINING DOS AND DON'TS

In 1922, the year in which The Great Gatsby *is set, early-twentieth-century manners expert Emily Post wrote a book that has become a classic as well. The book is* Etiquette: The Blue Book of Social Usage. *Post's dos and don'ts for social settings can be applied to any gathering.*

DO	DON'T
Say "present"	Say "introduce"
In a formal greeting, say "How do you do?"	Call out "Hello," and only extend this greeting between close friends.
In an informal greeting, say "How are you?" or "Good morning."	Dress dowdy. "A frumpy party is nothing more nor less than a collection of badly dressed persons. People with all the brains, even all the beauty imaginable, make an assemblage of dowds, unless they are well dressed."
For men: Remove hats when a woman enters the elevator. Place the hat back after exiting the elevator.	Use crude expressions like "My Gawd!" or "Wouldn't that jar you!"
For men: Rise when a lady walks into the room.	Use bad grammar. "People who say 'I come,' and 'I seen it,' and 'I done it' prove by their lack of grammar that they had little education in their youth."
For men: When in public, rise when a lady makes a remark or asks a question.	
For men: When a lady drops something, pick it up and mention it to the lady.	
For men: Tip the hat when passing by a lady.	

PLAYLIST

"It Had to Be You"

"Toot Toot Tootsie"

"Tea for Two"

"When You're Smiling"

"Ain't Misbehavin'"

"Singin' in the Rain"

"I Wanna Be Loved by You"

"Yes Sir, That's My Baby"

"Baby Face"

"Makin' Whoopie"

"Bye Bye Blackbird"

TOP SONGS OF 1925

"The Charleston"

"Sweet Georgia Brown"

"Sugar Foot Stomp"

"Careless Love Blues"

"I'll See You in My Dreams"

BOOK TRIVIA

1. How are the sandwiches described that Tom orders during the party at the apartment in the city?

a. Celebrated sandwiches
b. Deli sandwiches
c. Big, beefy sandwiches
d. Decadent sandwiches
e. Classic sandwiches

2. How are the hors d'oeuvres at Gatsby's poolside party described?

a. Splashy
b. The bee's knees
c. Glistening
d. Sparkly
e. Shiny

3. What are Daisy and Tom drinking with the cold fried chicken?

a. Two bottles of ale
b. Pale ale
c. Lemonade
d. Iced tea
e. Water

4. How many lemon cakes does Nick buy for Jay Gatsby's tea for Daisy?

a. 15
b. 12
c. 10
d. 5
e. 1

5. What drinks are served when Jay and Tom have lunch in the city?

a. Martinis
b. Highballs
c. Manhattans
d. Bee's Knees
e. French 75

ANSWERS: 1. a, 2. c, 3. a, 4. b, 5. b

BIBLIOGRAPHY

BOOKS & ARTICLES

"Appetizing menus for the week (Lemon Cake recipe)." *The Indianapolis Star.* April 5, 1925.

Bergstein, Rachelle. "The Waldorf is closing, but its salad lives on." *The New York Times.* February 21, 2017.

Bryer, Jackson R. and Barks, Cathy W. Dear Scott, Dearest Zelda: *The Love Letters of F. Scott and Zelda Fitzgerald.* Bloomsbury Publishing, LTD. 2003.

Castle, Sheri. "The history behind the legendary Lady Baltimore Cake." *Southern Living* magazine. August 7, 2022.

Donahue, Deirdre. *"'The Great Gatsby' by the numbers."* USA Today. May 7, 2013.

"Favorite dishes of favorite actresses (Julia Arthur Salad recipe)." *The Times.* March 11, 1917.

Fitzgerald, F. Scott. *A Short Autobiography.* Scribner. 2011.

Fitzgerald, F. Scott. "The Curious Case of Benjamin Button." *Collier's* magazine. May 27, 1922.

Fitzgerald, F. Scott. *The Great Gatsby.* C. Scribner's Sons. 1925.

Fitzgerald, F. Scott. *This Side of Paradise.* C. Scribner's Sons. 1920.

Fowler, Therese Anne. Z: *A Novel of Zelda Fitzgerald.* St. Martin's Griffin. 2014.

"Friday "Food Forum: How to use alligator pears." *The Evening Sun.* April 24, 1925.

"Frozen salad recipes for summer days (Tomato Ice Salad)." *Atlantic City Daily Press.* August 15, 1925.

Frozen Tomato Salad recipe. *The Richmond Item.* July 17, 1925.

Hazelgrove, William Elliott. *Writing Gatsby: The Real Story of the Writing of the Greatest American Novel.* Lyons Press. 2022.

"Lazy Daisy Cake." *The Fresno Morning Republican.* March 24, 1925.

Marshall, Mary. "What every woman wants to know (Fruit Cocktail recipe)." *The News Journal.* August 28, 1925.

Merriman, Woodene. "Pineapple Upside Down Cake catches 'wave'." *Pittsburgh Post-Gazette.* July 16, 1995.

Morton, Mrs. "Household hints (Peach and Cheese Salad recipe)." *Meriden Record.* August 25, 1925.

"Oriental Punch (recipe)" *Springfield News-Sun.* July 30, 1925.

"Peach Salad (recipe)." *Cincinnati Enquirer.* July 17, 1925.

Robuck, Erica. Call Me Zelda. Penguin Group. 2013.

Skeezix. "Lemon cake." *Daily Kennebec Journal.* October 8, 1928.

"Strawberry Whip (recipe)" *Charlotte Observer.* August 22, 1925.

"The Business of The Housewife, Recipes for fall canning (Pickled Carrots recipe)." *Seattle Union Record.* August 24, 1920.

"Timely Receipts (Pork Chops, Apple Sauce recipes)." *The Miami Herald.* September 30, 1922.

"Tomorrow's Menu (Consommé Madrilene recipe)." *Los Angeles Times.* June 10, 1925.

Weaver, Louise Bemmell. "The Housekeeper's Helper (Cranberry Fluff recipe by Louisa Grace." *Des Moines Tribune.* January 30, 1920.

Will-Weber, Mark. Mint Juleps with Teddy Roosevelt. Regnery History. 2014.

Woolworth lunch counter advertisement. *Atlantic City Daily Press.* April 2, 1925.

BLOGS

"Arnold Reuben: New York Restaurateur." *CooksInfo.com*

"F. Scott Fitzgerald in Minnesota." *AuthorAdventures.org*

"F. Scott Fitzgerald walking tour." *ExploreMinnesota.com*

"Our history." *TheKnickerbockerHotel.com*

New York Public Library, Menu, *Hotel Biltmore,* January 3, 1918

New York Public Library, Menu, *Hotel Biltmore,* May 23, 1925

"Oysters Rockefeller recipe and history." *WhatsCookingAmerica .net*

Schorow, Stephanie. "The legend of Ward 8." *EdibleBoston.com*

Shutte, Sue. "Peter Cooper & Jell-O." *NJ.gov*

Steinkellner, Kit. "Eating breakfast like Zelda Fitzgerald is a terrible idea. But I had to try it anyway." *MyRecipes.com.* February 13, 2018

"The story of the French 75 cocktail." *RevelryTours.com*

ACKNOWLEDGMENTS

Sincere gratitude to the many people who in some way were instrumental in this book project: Kelly Alexis, Edward Ash-Milby, Susan Wiencek, Keith Biesack, Debra-Ann Brabazon, Joanna Broder, Sara Burrows, Janna Childs, Bruce Conard, Mary Corrado, Barbara Culhane, Alicia Dale, Sheryl DeVore, Carol Dorava, Katherine Ferrera, Marc Foley, Mary Graham, Janice Harper, Bill Hinke, Dave Hinke, Elaine Hinke, Jeanne Hinke, Jeff Hinke, Jim Hinke, Shirley Hinke, Katie Killebrew, Kayla Kohlmeister, Robert Kowalski, Woody Leake, Chris Luebbe, Paul McPolin, Ann Michlig, Catherine Mio Anderson, Tim Moriarty, Joyce Nick, Alex Novak, Nityia Przewlocki, Ruth L. Ratny, Keith Rosenow, Kimberly Rosenow, Jenny Thomas, Cathy Tréboux, Greg Venne, Joel Weber, Susan Wiencek, Marilee Wright, David Yake.

ABOUT THE AUTHOR

 Veronica Hinke is a culinary and lifestyles journalist and instructor specializing in early-19th century drinking, dining, and entertainment. She is the author of *The Last Night on the Titanic: Unsinkable Drinking, Dining & Style*, *Titanic: The Official Cookbook*, and *Harry Potter Afternoon Tea Magic*.

INDEX

Index ❖ **133**

weldon**owen**

an imprint of Insight Editions

PO Box 3088
San Rafael, CA 94912
www.weldonowen.com

CEO Raoul Goff
Publisher Roger Shaw
Publishing Director Katie Killebrew
Executive Editor Edward Ash-Milby
Editorial Assistant Kayla Belser
VP Creative Chrissy Kwasnik
Designer Leah Lauer
VP Manufacturing Alix Nicholaeff
Sr Production Manager Joshua Smith
Sr Production Manager, Subsidiary Rights Lina s Palma-Temena

Weldon Owen would also like to thank Karen Levy
Photography Waterbury Publications, Inc.
Food Stylist Jennifer Peterson

ISBN: 979-8-88674-141-4

Manufactured in China by Insight Editions

10 9 8 7 6 5 4 3 2 1

ROOTS of PEACE   REPLANTED PAPER

Insight Editions, in association with Roots of Peace, will plant two trees
for each tree used in the manufacturing of this book. Roots of Peace
is an internationally renowned humanitarian organization dedicated to
eradicating land mines worldwide and converting war-torn lands into
productive farms and wildlife habitats. Roots of Peace will plant two
million fruit and nut trees in Afghanistan and provide farmers there with
the skills and support necessary for sustainable land use.